G000110154

THE
HONG KONG GUIDE
1893

THE
HONG KONG
GUIDE
1893

WITH AN INTRODUCTION BY
H.J. LETHBRIDGE

HONG KONG
OXFORD UNIVERSITY PRESS
OXFORD NEW YORK TOKYO
1982

Oxford University Press

Oxford London Glasgow
New York Toronto Melbourne Auckland
Kuala Lumpur Singapore Hong Kong Tokyo
Delhi Bombay Calcutta Madras Karachi
Nairobi Dar es Salaam Cape Town Salisbury

and associates in
Beirut Berlin Ibadan Mexico City Nicosia

First published by Kelly and Walsh, Limited, Shanghai, 1893.
This edition reprinted, with permission, by Oxford University Press, 1982.

This edition © Oxford University Press 1982

All rights reserved. No part of this publication may be reproduced,
stored in a retrieval system, or transmitted, in any form or by any
means, electronic, mechanical, photocopying, recording or otherwise,
without the prior permission of Oxford University Press.

ISBN 0 19 581503 3

Cover design by Colin Tillyer.
Printed in Hong Kong.
Published by Oxford University Press, Warwick House,
Quarry Bay, Hong Kong

INTRODUCTION

*K*elly and Walsh's Handbook to Hong Kong, so described in the *Hong Kong Government Gazette*, first appeared on the bookstalls in May 1893. The public paid a dollar for its 160-odd pages of information and advertisements. A 1,000 copies were printed. The author, whose name does not appear on the title-page, is given as one 'Bruce Shepherd'. There were two Bruce Shepherds in Hong Kong at that time. The first was Librarian to the Supreme Court; the other was Clerk of the Deed Registry at the same institution. Both had lived in the Colony for over a decade and, one surmises, knew the highways and byways of Hong Kong intimately, a Hong Kong which did not include, at that date, the New Territories. Since office hours in those less hurried days were from ten until four, with an interruption for a long tiffin at noon, each had plenty of time to compile this guide.

There must have been in the 1890's a brisk demand for such compilations, for both William Legge's *Guide to Hong Kong* (3,000 copies) and Sydney Skertchly's *Our Island* (1,000 copies) also appeared in 1893. Other guides could be mentioned. It is clear that enterprising local publishers and printers were aiming not at the resident European population, then numbering only a few thousand, but at the stream — a torrent at times — of travellers, tourists and globe-trotters, coming in increasing numbers to Imperial Britain's far distant outpost, the great port, entrepôt and naval base of Hong Kong. General Ulysses Grant, the ex-President of the United States, on his much-publicized world cruise, made landfall at Hong Kong in 1879 and was welcomed by the Governor himself. The young Kipling stopped over at Hong Kong in 1889 and wrote about his experiences.

Travel to the East became relatively easy for those with wanderlust when the Peninsula and Oriental

Steamship Navigation Company introduced a monthly line of mail steamers to Hong Kong via India in the 1840's. In 1863 the French Messageries Maritime began to operate between Europe and the Far East, and in 1867 the Pacific Mail Steamship Company linked San Francisco with Yokohama and Hong Kong. By the 1890's then, Hong Kong was part of a world-wide network of shipping services. It was a port of call for nearly all ocean liners coming to the East. As a consequence, thousands of tourists and travellers came to Hong Kong every year, some of whom made side-trips to Macau, Canton and other parts of China. This inspired the construction of numerous luxury hotels and hostelries in Hong Kong, and the more prestigious of them bought advertising space in the Guide, such as the Hong Kong Hotel and the Mount Austin Hotel up on the Peak. A demand for guidebooks of Hong Kong had been created; Bruce Shepherd was one of a number of local authors who catered for that need.

Guidebooks as a class form a minor literary genre. They date from the nineteenth century, the age of locomotion (although, of course, examples may be found pre-dating that great transitional epoch). In 1836 John Murray, the celebrated London publisher, issued the first of his guides for travellers, *Holland, Belgium, and the Rhine*. 'Murray's Handbooks', in their familiar red cloth bindings, became standard equipment for the British traveller in Europe and the Near East. George Bradshaw, a shrewd Manchester printer, published his first railway guide in 1839; in 1847 he brought out a continental railway guide. The German publisher, Karl Baedeker, inspired by Murray, instituted his own series in the 1840's. These guidebooks were designed initially for the traveller in Europe. But as Europeans, and then Americans, started to venture further afield, as communications improved, to India, the Malay archipelago, China and Japan, the ambit of such guides grew. Guidebooks became international: all accessible countries were described, however perfunctorily.

Guidebooks, needless to say, throw light on the compiler and, in broad terms, on the contemporary culture that envelops or engulfs him. What does he include and what does he leave out? It was, for example, standard practice for a Victorian author of a guide to Paris to present a detailed description of the Paris morgue, then open to visitors. Every European visitor to Canton was expected to visit the city's execution ground, where Chinese felons were publicly beheaded. Was this an expression of Victorian England's obsession with death and funerary rites?

Bruce Shepherd sets the tone of his guidebook in his introduction. He declares: 'No apology can be necessary for offering a Handbook to the British Crown Colony of Hong Kong. For ages prior to the year 1841, it existed only as a plutonic island of uninviting sterility, apparently capable only of supporting the lowest forms of organisms. To-day, it stands forth before the world with its City of Victoria and a permanent population of over two hundred thousand souls — a noble monument to British pluck and enterprise.'

The modern reader should find this passage perplexing since it suggests Hong Kong had *no* history before 1841, the year the British took possession. This cannot be so because records, historical and archaeological, reveal that Hong Kong supported a settled population of farmers, fishermen and other Chinese, dating back at least to the Sung Dynasty and the twelfth century. There is, it follows, a pre-British history of Hong Kong — a Chinese history — and this has been established by, among other scholars, Professor Lo Hsiang-lin and S.F. Balfour. Certainly, Hong Kong's rocky terrain did not encourage opulence or a leisured class; the islanders were always poor and few, if any, ever became scholars. Bruce Shepherd refers (ironically?) to the 'lowest forms of organisms.' Presumably, on his evolutionary scale, the 'highest forms' were taipans and clubmen, and perhaps a few extremely rich Chinese. Finally, no one speaks today of the 'City of Victoria'. This designation has vanished. Urban Hong Kong is simply termed 'Hong Kong' or 'Central'.

Bruce Shepherd, like all of us, was a man of his time. His guidebook celebrates Imperial progress and English (British) institutions. The Chinese are mentioned only occasionally and then usually derisively. His readers are expected to view and admire the Peak with its European habitations, European amenities and social atmosphere. As he writes: 'The visitor will probably select Victoria Peak as the first place of interest after his arrival in Hong Kong ...'. Government House, and other public buildings, the Anglican and Catholic Cathedrals, Union Church, Victoria Prison and Magistracy, are all given prominence in his account. So, too, are the Happy Valley Race Course, the Botanical Gardens, the Hong Kong Club, the larger hotels and the docks. Several paragraphs are devoted to the system of water catchments and reservoirs, symbolic of the High Victorian craze for good sanitation and clean water. All these buildings and places were intimately linked with the British presence in Hong Kong and were inspired by British conceptions of how a city should be organized.

Bruce Shepherd was proud of Hong Kong's 50 years or so of progress — the text makes this amply clear — but natural pride in British achievements made him undervalue Chinese contributions. All the public and other notable buildings had been built by Chinese labour, and Chinese artisans and craftsmen decorated them or fitted them out. Chinese merchants played a key, and in time dominant, role in the young Colony's economic and commercial success. Mention is made at times, it is true, of Chinese temples and houses or Chinese villages; but the reader is always directed more to the British or European side of things. This, surely, distinguishes Kelly and Walsh's 1893 Guide from the type of literature now put out by the Hong Kong Tourist Association. Today, visitors are likely to seek the Chinese component in many-layered Hong Kong. It is odd, for example, that no mention is made of Chinese cuisine, regarded as the best in the world. Odder still is the lack of any detailed reference to Chinese shops, especially the many curio shops that always welcomed foreign custom and supplied the traveller with interesting bric-à-brac, fabulous gewgaws and keepsakes, as they continue to do in contemporary Hong Kong.

This brings us back again to the author, to the personality or character of the 'Bruce Shepherd' who was, we cannot be certain which, either Clerk or Librarian at the Supreme Court. The anonymous author leaves his footprints in this text and scatters clues. It seems not implausible to suggest he was of lower middle-class origin and probably a Scot (Britain's former colonial possessions were mainly staffed by Scots). He was a somewhat puritanical and priggish chap. He refers to gamblers as 'canaille'; has contempt for hearty eating and drinking at picnics; scoffs at men who refuse to go on long walks; is caustic about those in a past era who sported a carriage and liked to perambulate in it; he always has a dig at pretension. He appears a serious man. Was he a muscular Christian, a devoted believer in *mens sana in corpore sano*? One thing is certain; he was a great, and possibly heroic, walker.

Embedded in the mass of detail — the guidebook side of the publication — are several curious stories. I refer the reader to the mysterious murder of Lieutenant Da Costa and friend at Wong-ma Kok (rumour later had it that a drunken Da Costa had assaulted a village maiden and had been killed by her outraged relatives); the 'haunted house' at Happy Valley, haunted, according to the legend, because three Jardines directors died there in the space of 18 months. One only wishes Bruce Shepherd had given us more gleanings from his memories of Hong Kong. Doubtless he had many tales to tell of scandal and intrigue — but a guidebook is not expected to drift too far into yellow journalism. As it is, his guide stands up well after all these years, with its vintage quaintness and quirks.

H.J. LETHBRIDGE

BIBLIOGRAPHY

Balfour, S.F., 'Hong Kong Before the British', *Journal of the Hong Kong Branch of the Royal Asiatic Society*, 10 (1970), 134-79.

Dictionary of National Biography (Article on John Murray, publisher).

Eitel, E.J., *Europe in China: The History of Hong Kong From the Beginning to the Year 1882* (Hong Kong: Kelly and Walsh, 1895).

Endacott, G.B., *A History of Hong Kong* (London: Oxford University Press, 1958).

Kipling, Rudyard, *From Sea to Sea, and Other Sketches* (London: Macmillan, 1900).

Lo, Hsiang-lin, *Hong Kong and Its External Communications Before 1842. The History of Hong Kong Prior to British Arrival* (Hong Kong: Institute of Chinese Culture, 1963).

Norton-Kyshe, James William, *The History of the Laws and Courts of Hong Kong From the Earliest Period to 1898* (London: T. Fisher Unwin, 1898).

Young, John Russell, *Round the World With General Grant* (New York: American News Company, 1879).

A

HAND-BOOK

TO

HONGKONG.

BEING

A POPULAR GUIDE TO THE VARIOUS PLACES OF INTEREST
IN THE COLONY, FOR THE USE OF TOURISTS.

———————

HONGKONG:

KELLY & WALSH, LIMITED,

AND AT

SHANGHAI, YOKOHAMA AND SINGAPORE.

1893.

(All Rights Reserved).

INTRODUCTION.

No apology can be necessary for offering a Hand-book to the British Crown Colony of Hong-kong. For ages prior to the year 1841, it existed only as a plutonic island of uninviting sterility, apparently capable only of supporting the lowest forms of organisms. To-day, it stands forth before the world with its City of Victoria and a permanent population of over two hundred thousand souls—a noble monument to British pluck and enterprise. From its position on the south-eastern shores of the continent of Asia and the great Chinese Empire, to which it originally belonged—and to which it is still supposed to belong by thousands of Chinese who daily throng the native portions of the City—its roads and buildings constructed at enormous cost, owing to the steep and rocky nature of the ground; the variety of its inhabitants from all the quarters of the globe; its magnificent land-locked harbour, and its reliance for its very existence upon the shipping which is continually entering the harbour from the principal countries and ports of the world—Hongkong is of surpassing interest as a British possesion, and its influence upon the future of the neighbouring Empire, it is difficult, if not impossible to foretell. No stranger, however unsympathetic, can pass along the roads and streets of Hongkong without a feeling of wonder and admiration at the almost magical influence, which in so few years, could transform the barren granite mountain sides of the island of Hongkong into one of the most pleasant cities of the earth. Hongkong is the most eastern station of the British Empire on the voyage round the world, and is the point of union with the splendid mail steamers of England, France, and Germany from Europe and the East, with the equally magnificent mail steamers which leave Hongkong eastward for Canada and the United States, and south-easterly for Australasia. In addition, Hongkong possesses banking and telegraph facilities to every place in the world.

The design of this little work is to give a succinct description of Hongkong, its history, interesting objects and excursions, with notes of the Climate, Sanitation, Flora and Fauna of the Colony, sufficient to afford the visitor some additional information and pleasure from his visit, and it is hoped that the older residents of the Colony may also derive some pleasant reminiscences from the chapters on the excursions to the different places on the island and mainland adjacent.

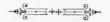

CONTENTS.

—: ❋ :—

CHAPTER I.

CHAPTER II.

CHAPTER III.

CHAPTER VI.

CHAPTER V.

CHAPTER VI.

CHAPTER VII.

CHAPTER VIII.

CHAPTER XI.

CHAPTER X.

CHAPTER XI.

CHAPTER XII.

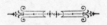

THE HONGKONG GUIDE.

CHAPTER I.

GENERAL DESCRIPTION.

Geographical Position of Hongkong Island.—The British Crown Colony
of Hongkong.—Description of the Island.—Dominating Position as
regards South China.—Hongkong Harbour.—Origin of the Name.

HONGKONG is an island situated off the South-eastern
coast of the empire of China and immediately adjacent
to the mainland. Hongkong, with its dependencies
(which include a part of the mainland known as the Kowloon
Peninsula, Stonecutters' Island and a few other small islands)
is a British Crown colony.

The island of Hongkong lies between 22° 10′ and 22° 17′
North latitude and 114° 6′ and 114° 18′ East longitude. It is
bounded on the North by the harbour of Victoria (also known as
Hongkong Harbour), on the North-east by the Lymoon Pass—
which is only from a quarter to half a mile wide—on the East
by Tathong Channel and on the South and West by the China
Sea—here studded with numerous islands and islets. Victoria
Harbour, Lymoon Pass, and Tathong Channel, separate the
island from the mainland of China within the province of
Kwangtung.

A

The island of Hongkong has a circumference of 27 miles
and an area of 30 square miles, its length is about 11 miles
and its breadth from two to five miles. The greater part of the
island is mountainous. Indeed the North side of the island is
separated from the South by a continuous range of high and
abrupt hills terminating in rocky peaks mostly upwards of 1,000
feet above the sea level, while Victoria Peak on the West side—
where the maritime signal station is situated—and Mount
Parker on the East side are from 1,820 to 1,840 feet high, with
steep descents to the sea. The average width of the western
half of the island is only three miles and the descent from the
hills to the sea is consequently very abrupt and precipitous.
The eastern division of the island is much wider, the ridges
of high hills extending more to the North, and also a greater
distance to the South, so that the extreme width of the island,
about seven miles, is there obtained. The south-eastern part
of the island is divided, however, by an inlet of the sea, a
mile and a half broad, for the greater part, and running for
three miles between the hills, called Taitam Bay. This Bay
forms the south-eastern side of the island into two peninsulas,
known as the Taitam and D'Aguilar peninsulas.

All the hills are thickly strewn with huge granite boulders,
black with age and exposure to the weather. Numerous ravines,
worked out by the torrents occasioned by the heavy summer
rains, furrow the hill sides and give them a worn and rather
desolate appearance.

During heavy rains, which happen in the summer season,
all the ravines are turned into torrents; but in the winter
season, when comparatively little rain falls, the ravines are
generally dry. There is a curious and even remarkable
exception, however, in some few of the ravines which are
channels for streamlets, furnishing continually a good supply

of water, and not failing in the driest season, when all others are dried up.

The indentations between the higher hills are called gaps. From the western gap known as Victoria Gap, at an elevation of 1,200 feet above sea level, run two deep and extremely picturesque ravines; the one in a southerly direction, terminates at the suburb af Pokfulam and includes the Pokfulam Reservoir for supplying water to the city of Victoria, three miles distant; the other ravine takes a northerly direction to the eastern division of the city. From the Wongneichung Gap again, three miles farther East than Victoria Gap, run two more deep ravines; one in a south-easterly direction terminating at Taitam Bay and the other in a northerly direction terminating in the valley of Wongneichung, also known as the Happy Valley around which is the Race-course. Many more ravines have been formed by the mountain torrents both on the North and South sides of the island and are highly picturesque, particularly when viewed from the higher hills.

The surface of the island is mostly disintegrated or decomposed granite, red earth, and hard rock, but beds of clay are found in several places, even on the tops of some of the higher hills. Embedded in the red earth are huge round boulders of hard blue stone and grey granite, the latter having the quartz, mica, and felspar well proportioned and of the best description for building purposes. The granite quarries of Hongkong Island and Kowloon are exceedingly valuable and form a considerable item in the revenue of the Colony.

Standing on the northern slopes of the island and looking North across the harbour to the mainland, mountainous ridges are seen running nearly East and West, the highest point of which is the peak of Taimoshan (great military watch mountain) about 3,000 feet high. These ridges, which shut out the view

A 2

of the mainland to the North, are an outcrop of the Yu Ling mountains which stretch across the provinces of Kwong Tung and Kwong Si. At the foot of this ridge and to the East of Taimoshan, is seen the peninsula of Kowloon running into the northern portion of the harbour and opposite the eastern portion of the city of Victoria. The peninsula of Kowloon is about two miles and-a-half in length and two miles across along the boundary line dividing British Kowloon from Chinese territory, but comprises an area of three square miles only, by excluding Hung Hom Bay running into the southern portion of the Peninsula and Tokwa Bay on its eastern side. The distance from the most southerly point of Kowloon, known as Kowloon Point or Tsim Sha Tsui (Sharp Sand Point), to Hongkong Island is $1\frac{1}{8}$ miles. The Kowloon peninsula consists to a large extent of low ranges of rugged hills of a very confused nature, some of the hills being absolutely sterile, but containing large and valuable masses of granite, chiefly in hugh boulders.

From its geographical position Hongkong commands the estuary of the Canton river and therefore the entrance into the great empire of China from the South. Hongkong is 90 miles from Canton—the capital of Southern China. The position of Hongkong as regards the South coast of China can well be observed from Victoria Peak which is 1,825 feet above the sea level. From this spot, on a clear day, the estuary of the Canton river can be seen to the North-west over the north-eastern portion of an island known as Lan Tau, the high peak of a mountain on the mainland known as Castle Peak, forming its south-eastern boundary.

The City of Victoria stands at the foot of Victoria Peak and on the lower slopes of its northern side. The chief entrance to the city from the harbour is at Peddar's Wharf, in the very centre of the European portion of the city. The direct entrance to the harbour from Europe and the South is on the western side of Hongkong Island, and from Australasia, America, Japan and North China, the entrance is on the eastern side along the northern shore of the island and through Lymoon Pass.

As Hongkong Island is approached by steamer from the South, it is difficult to distinguish it from the mountainous country of the mainland, nor is there any apparent difference in its barren looking appearance, between it and other hilly islands which appear to surround it, except that some houses and buildings of European style may be observed on the hill side at Pokfulam and the mast on Victoria Peak is signalling the ship to those in the city below, on the other side. The channel leading along the western side of Hongkong into the harbour is known as Sulphur Channel and the small island, between which and Hongkong island the channel is formed, is Green Island, upon which stands one of the three lighthouses marking the entrances to the harbour. The steamer, having passed through Sulphur Channel, gradually rounds the north-western side of Hongkong and turning East into the harbour discovers a scene of life and activity, as well as natural beauty, which calls forth the greatest admiration. Overlooking the harbour is the city of Victoria, extending along the northern shore of the island for upwards of four miles, its buildings carried back and up the steep slope of the mountain, tier beyond tier, in some cases to charming situations 600 feet above the sea level. In the harbour and alongside the wharves at Kowloon are seen steamers of all nationalities loading or discharging cargo. Among the steamers frequently to be seen in the harbour at one time, are the magnificent mail steamers of the Canadian Pacific Railway, and of the Pacific Mail, Messageries Maritimes, Peninsular and Oriental, and North German Lloyds Steamship Companies. Other steamers may be recognized by their house flags and funnels, those of the Ocean line have blue funnels; the red funnels belong to the Indo-China, the Glen, or the Scottish Oriental lines of steamers. Junks, of all descriptions and too numerous to be counted, are lying in rows alongside the Praya or sea-wall from which long lines of coolies with bamboos are carrying the cargo to or from the warehouses, called godowns. Junks, already laden with cargo, have hoisted their huge mat sails, and with cannon pointed—to show the pirates they are prepared to fight—are threading their way through the harbour on their way to some Chinese port where foreign vessels are not allowed to trade, and as they depart crackers are fired, gongs are beaten, and joss papers burnt to the sea deities who will have them in their care until their arrival at their destination. The man-of-war anchorage is on the eastern side of the harbour along the Hongkong shore and here, during the winter and spring months, may be seen war ships, gunboats, and cruisers of the China squadrons of Great Britain, Russia, France, the United States, China and Japan, and occasionally the representative ships of Austria, Spain, and Portugal. Numerous steam-launches of every description appear to be hurrying across the harbour in every direction and give an animation to the scene which cannot be met with in any other Port. Looking in an easterly direction the barren looking and precipitous hills of the mainland are seen converging with the most northern hills of Hongkong until they close in and form the comparatively narrow Lymoon Pass which constitutes the eastern entrance to Hongkong harbour. Looking across the harbour to the West is seen the island of Lan-tao, distant about ten miles, with mountainous peaks and shutting in the view on that side. The harbour of Hongkong appears therefore to be almost land-locked and as seen from some positions has the appearance of a beautiful lake of from one to five miles in width and ten miles in length. The geographical position of Hongkong, commanding as it does the entrance to South China, is well observed from the signal station at Victoria Peak. On a clear day the mainland with its mountainous ridges can be seen for many miles, the highest mountain visible being Ma-on Shan, which is more than 4,000 feet high. The trend of the coast to the North-east can be followed until it is lost to view in the dim horizon, the island of Pedro Blanco, distance 50 miles, is plainly visible in moderately clear weather. To the North-west, to the left of Castle Peak, can be seen the broad waters of the Canton river leading away to the North and the entrance to which, on this side, is through the narrow passage to the North-west, which is known as the Capsingmun Pass.

To the West and South are the islands and islets fringing the coast of China as far as the eye can reach. The dominating position of Hongkong is also strikingly observed by those arriving from the Canton river to Hongkong through the Capsingmun Pass, when Victoria Peak, with the whole of the western portion of Hongkong island, comes into view and appears, from its commanding mass, as the lord of this portion of the earth. When Sir George Bowen was Governor of Hongkong he gave to Hongkong the name of the Gibraltar and Malta of the Far East and no doubt from the North-western portion of the harbour the view of Hongkong accords with this comparison. But Hongkong is *sui generis*, and comparisons, alone, will fail to convey to the mind of the visitor the position and importance of Hongkong to the mighty empire to which it is the southern gate.

The name of Hongkong, as given to the island, is not very clear and has given rise to some discussion. The name by which it was known to the Chinese was Kwan-tai-lo (Petticoat String Road) which may have arisen from the original ribbon-like road or pathway along the northern shore or from the ribbon-like passages along which the island was passed by the junks on their way from the eastern coast ports to Canton. The characters used by the Chinese for Hong Kong (香 港 Heung Kong) mean literally "Fragrant Sea Port," but are sometimes translated "Fragrant Streams" the sound 江 Kong, a stream being mistaken for the sound 港 Kong, a sea-port; the latter of which alone is properly applied to Hongkong; the character for sea port may, however, have been applied to the sound of Kong or stream. The merchant ships of the East India Company frequently took in water from a stream running into the sea on the South side of the island between Pokfulam and Aberdeen. This stream falls over a basaltic rock into a small bay and forms during the wet season a most picturesque waterfall from which the bay is called Waterfall Bay. The water of this stream had long been known for its excellence, and it was customary for Chinese junks and piratical craft to get their water supply from this source and it may well be that the waterfall so easily accessible was called Heung Kong or fragrant streams, and that the name (although not the Chinese characters) was afterwards given to the whole island. Hongkong was classed by the ancient Portuguese as one of the Ladrones (Thieves) islands by reason of the numerous islands fringing the coast and the entrance to the Canton river, being the abodes of pirates who made these islands their strongholds. Although the island of Hongkong has been for a long time excluded from the group of Ladrone islands, the group of islands to the South and South-west are still known by that name, the Great Ladrone (rising 2,000 feet above sea level), 30 miles South of Hongkong, being the first land sighted by ships coming from the South to Hongkong.

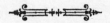

CHAPTER II.

HISTORY OF HONGKONG.

Early History.—Hongkong in 1816.—British Trade with China.—East India Company's Monopoly.—End of Monopoly and Appointment of Lord Napier, Chief Superintendent.—Lord Napier's death.—Mr. J. F. Davis and Sir George B. Robinson, Chief Superintendents.—Quiescent Policy of Sir George B. Robinson.—Appointment of Captain Elliot as Superintendent.—Arrival of Admiral Sir Frederick Maitland.—Affairs at Canton.—Edicts against Opium Trade.—Imprisonment of the Merchants at Canton.—Destruction of Opium.—Captain Elliot and Merchants retire to Macao.

THE antiquarian will find but little to interest him within the limits of Hongkong. The Colony has grown to its present position and importance within the last half century, as the result of the necessities of English trade with China. The Colony was ceded to the British Crown in the year 1841 and prior to that date but little was known of the Island which has given its name to the Colony. The territory comprised within the boundaries of the Colony was formerly included within the district of San On of the maritime province of Kwangtung.

Formerly Canton was the only port to which foreign ships were allowed to come, and ships, in the old days, sailing to Canton from the South and East on their way to the Canton river, were attracted by the beautiful waterfall on the South side of the island of Hongkong then known as one of the Ladrones or Thieves Islands, and would stop to take in a supply of fresh water. The *Alceste* and *Lyra,* conveying Lord Amherst's embassy to China, with the East India Company's cruisers

Discovery and *Investigator*, conveying Sir George Staunton as second member of the Commission, and the Chinese secretaries and interpreters, anchored near this waterfall from the 10th to the 13th July, 1816, on their way North to the mouth of the Pei-ho. Professor Abel, who accompanied Lord Amherst's embassy, referring to the inhabitants of Hongkong at that time, stated that "none were seen but some poor and weather-beaten fishermen spreading their nets and drying the produce of their toils on the rocks which supported their miserable mud-huts." At this time, and until the year 1841, the site of the present City of Victoria was simply the rocky and bouldered lower slopes of the northern side of the mountain whose summit is known as Victoria Peak, these slopes in most cases descending precipitously into the waters of the harbour. The ships of the East India Company and Opium Clippers frequently anchored off Hongkong Island before proceeding up the river to Whampoa and Canton, but it was not till the year 1837 that the whole season's shipping resorted to Hongkong, and the position of the island and the secure anchorage around it came into prominence. It will not be out of place here to take a glance at the history of British trade with China which led to the first war with China and the cession of the island to the British Crown.

The East India Company had the monopoly of British trade with China for 200 years until the year 1833 when the Government determined that the trade, which was limited to the port of Canton, should be free, but should be carried on under the supervision of superintendents of trade, upon whom were to be conferred judicial powers for the administration of justice. Accordingly by Royal Commission, dated the 10th December, 1833, William John, Lord Napier was appointed Chief Superintendent of the trade with China, and in the following month received his instructions to proceed to Canton. With Lord Napier were associated Mr. W. H. C. Plowden and Mr. J. F. Davis, the senior supercargoes of the East India Company's service at Canton, as second and third superintendents of trade.

Lord Napier sailed for China in the frigate *Andromache* and arrived at Macao on the 15th July, 1834, where he found the select committee and supercargoes of the late East India Company's establishment, and Mr. Plowden being absent, Mr. J. F. Davis accepted the situation of second superintendent. On the 23rd the superintendents with their secretaries and interpreters proceeded on the *Andromache* to the anchorage at Chuenpee below the forts at Bocca Tigris, and as Lord Napier's instructions from Lord Palmerston were that no British ship of war should enter the Port of Canton, which was supposed to commence at the Bocca Tigris, the superintendents left the *Andromache* at Chuenpee and proceeded in a cutter to Canton, where they arrived on the 25th. Lord Napier at once, in accordance with Lord Palmerston's instructions, reported himself and his commission to the Viceroy of Canton. The Viceroy, however, refused to receive any communication from the barbarian " Eye," as the Chinese called Lord Napier from his apparently to them having only one name, and Loo, the Governor of Canton, directed the Hong merchants to ascertain why the barbarian Eye had come to Canton, why in disobedience to the regulations he had not requested a red permit, and ordering them to compel him immediately to return to Macao and reside there, and threatened that the trade should be stopped and commerce eternally cut off if he did not go from the city.

During the whole time the East India Company held the monopoly of British trade at Canton the officers of that Company, called Taipans, carried on all their communications with a syndicate of Chinese merchants, of whom Howqua and Mowqua were the chiefs, and had no direct access to the Chinese Government officers. The Hong merchants practically up to this period had governed not only the trade but the traders, although the great trade of the Company with Canton, amounting to some millions a year, gave the officer of the Company great influence over the merchants. It was the Hong merchants who in 1747 used every endeavour to prevent the access of strangers to the Government offices, and their success enabled them to impose upon their own Government as well as the foreign merchants with impunity.

Lord Napier insisted upon his right to present his letter to the Viceroy without the intervention of the Hong merchants and refused to leave Canton. The Hong merchants then on the 16th August announced the trade to be suspended, and no further change taking place, the Viceroy, on the 2nd September, officially announced all trade to be at an end between the Chinese and British subjects, ordered away all Chinese from the factories, placed a cordon of troops and boats to cut off all communication from Canton, and directed the Chinese not to supply either Lord Napier or his factory with provisions. Lord Napier thereupon sent to the frigates *Imogene* and *Andromache* at Chuenpee for assistance. These frigates forced the passage under the fire of the Chinese from the Bogue forts and the fort on Tiger island. One sailor was killed on each of the frigates but the loss to the Chinese was not ascertained. The frigates arrived at Whampoa but their presence there did not produce the effect upon the Chinese Government which Lord Napier expected, the Chinese authorities still adhering to the terms that Lord Napier should take his departure for Macao, and the frigates for Chuenpee, before trade would be allowed to be resumed. Lord Napier, finding that the opening of the trade depended upon his proceeding to Macao, resolved to leave Canton immediately. He was suffering from fever at the time and on account of the state of his health the Chinese Government allowed him to proceed to Macao by the inner passage in a chop boat, where he arrived on the 26th September, after unnecessary delays interposed on his passage down, and the trade was reopened at Canton on the 29th of the same month. Lord Napier never recovered but died on the 11th October following.

Mr. J. F. Davis succeeded Lord Napier as Chief Superintendent but remained at Macao unrecognized by the Chinese authorities. Pending the receipt of instructions from home, Mr. Davis carefully abstained from any steps calculated to pledge the English Government or to embarrass in any way whatever, the commercial transactions of individuals. He resigned the office of Chief Superintendent in January 1835, and Sir George Best Robinson thereupon assumed the office and duties of Chief Superintendent, Mr. Astell that of Second, and Captain Elliot, late Secretary, that of Third Superintendent.

On the same day that the new Superintendents assumed their duties, the 22nd January, 1835, the British ship *Argyle*, Captain Alexander Macdonald, bound from Bengal to Canton, had made St. John's Island and anchored in a harbour on the East coast. The Captain sent his mate, two helmsmen, and nine sailors in his boat to the shore with the intention of procuring a pilot who would guide his ship over the shoals to Macao. The inhabitants of St. John's were, however, unfortunately ruffians ; they captured the boat, took the mate and sailors prisoners, and then sent a demand to the Captain for $500 to bring the people back. Captain Macdonald had not the money with him and under all the circumstances he thought it best to make for Macao, where he arrived on the 29th. The three Superintendents, finding that those unfortunate men had fallen into the hands of some of the notoriously lawless people of the southern coast of China, determined

at once to report the circumstances direct to the principal
authorities at Canton. The report was drawn up and signed
by the three Superintendents and their seals affixed to their
signatures, and it was arranged that Captain Elliot should present
it at the water gate Canton, accompanied only by Mr. Gutzlaff
the interpreter and the Captain of the *Argyle*. On the 1st
February, Captain Elliot and his two companions reached Canton
and went to the landing place near the Yeu-lan gate which
leads to the Governor's palace. They had proceeded a short
distance only, when some Chinese soldiers suddenly appeared fell
upon Captain Elliot and struggled with him until he fell to
the ground. Captain Elliot, Macdonald, and the Interpreter
were then successively dragged though two wicket gates where
Captain Elliot presented the report to a military Mandarin, who
simply sneered at them and took off his upper robes as a sign
of contempt. Half an hour after this several Mandarins, all in
their State uniforms, arrived, and among them was Monqua the
senior Hong merchant. Two general officers, deputed by the
Governor, seated themselves in the Watch-house, the gates were
thrown open and Captain Elliot and his companions brought
into their presence. Captain Elliot then presented the document
to one of them but the Mandarin refused to receive it. The
Interpreter than explained that it was an urgent case concerning
the lives of twelve British subjects, but the Mandarins stated they
only received "Petitions" and withdrew. Captain Elliot and
his companions also withdrew and returned to their boat without
further molestation.

Notwithstanding the Mandarins would not receive the letter
from Captain Elliot, because it is was not a petition, the Canton
authorities are supposed to have acted upon the verbal intimation,
for the men were restored to their ship at Macao on the 26th
February.

Sir George Robinson persevered in his course of quiescent policy and towards the end of the year 1835 congratulated himself upon its apparent success and the uninterrupted tranquility and peace which prevailed, notwithstanding the discordant state of society and want of goodwill existing among the British community in China. In November, 1835, Sir George Robinson moved from Macao and came to reside at the anchorage of Lintin an island nearer to the Bogue forts. This he did in order to obviate the inconvenience and delay entailed upon the commanders of British ships and others by the necessity of repairing to Macao to obtain a port clearance before proceeding up the river to Whampoa. The change to Lintin gave universal satisfaction to everyone engaged on the trade to China and was the first step in obtaining a separate and independent position for the carrying on of the British trade with China. This position was in the outer waters, and the Chinese authorities did not interfere. It was also outside the jurisdiction of the Chinese and Portuguese authorities at Macao, and British ships could therefore, under the protection of British authorities, anchor under Lintin or, if necessary, in the harbours of the islands of Lantao and Hongkong, within easy reach.

The anchorage of Lintin, is so much exposed, however, during the southerly monsoon as to render it unsafe for the shipping in the tempestuous weather which sweeps over these seas during the summer months, and during the spring of the following year, 1836, it was considered desirable to remove the anchorage to the safe and commodious basin or harbour of Hongkong. The state of British society was unhappily at that time in so divided and irritable a state, that Sir George Robinson could do nothing but continue in his quiescent line of policy.

On the 14th December following, however, Sir George Robinson received a despatch from Lord Palmerston informing him that the office of Chief Superintendent had been abolished and directing him to make over the archives and documents of the establishment to Captain Elliot, R.N., which he at once did.

Captain Elliot the same day sent a communication to the Governor of Canton to inform him that he had been appointed by the English Government as Chief English Authority in China, and to request permission to come to Canton to reside and fulfil his duties. This communication bore the Chinese character *Pin* (a petition from an inferior) as a superscription and was sent to the Hong merchants to be forwarded to the Governor (Tang).

This communication the Governor received and acknowledged through the Hong merchants, who were requested to inform Captain Elliot that he must remain at Macao until his communication had been reported to the throne.

On the 18th March, 1837, the Imperial sanction for the residence of Captain Elliot at Canton was communicated by the Hoppo on condition that he conformed to the old regulations by residing at Macao when the season was finished and not loitering in Canton beyond the proper period, and upon the receipt of this sanction Captain Elliot forthwith took up his official residence at Canton.

At this time piracies were frequent, not only in and about Canton, but in the neighbourhood of Macao, and arrangements were made for one or more ships of war on the East India station to proceed to a convenient station in Chinese waters in communication with the Superintendent.

During this year also the Emperor of China had directed reports to be made on the opium trade and finally directed that the most stringent measures should be adopted to stop the trade entirely, and all merchants and merchants' vessels dealing in opium to be removed beyond the outer waters of the Celestial Empire.

Accordingly, on the 29th September, 1837, the local authorities of Canton called upon Captain Elliot to drive away all the merchants and merchants' vessels dealing in opium, but this Captain Elliot replied was beyond his powers as Superintendent; the vessels were anchored out of his jurisdiction, and, according to the edict of the Governor, had permanently anchored at Whampoa, Lin Tin, and other land-locked places since the year 1821.

In November, 1837, a despatch was received by Captain Elliot, from Lord Palmerston, directing him to discontinue the use of the character *Pin* on his addresses to the Governor of Canton; but upon Captain Elliot informing the Governor of his instructions, the Governor declined to accede to the conditions and Captain Elliot thereupon withdrew to Macao.

On the 13th July, 1838, Admiral Sir Frederick L. Maitland arrived off Macao in Her Majesty's ship *Wellesley*, 74, accompanied by the *Algerine*. Captain Elliot immediately joined the Admiral and proceeded outwards with the ships to the anchorage of Tong Koo Bay, distant about seven leagues south of the Bocca Tigris, and remote from the anchorage of the ships engaged in the illicit opium traffic. Captain Elliot then endeavoured to address the Governor of Canton for the purpose of acquainting him with the peaceful visit of one of Her Majesty's ships, but the Governor stated the orders from the Emperor were imperative and he could receive no communication unless it bore the character *Pin*.

During this correspondence, Captain Middlemist of the British ship *Falcon*, proceeded from Hongkong, where his ship was lying, in the schooner *Bombay* (passage boat) for Canton, and, when passing the Bogue, the batteries fired several shots at the boat, which was at last boarded by a Mandarin's officer, who inquired if Admiral Maitland or any of his soldiers, women, or man-of-war's men were on board, and being answered in the

B

negative, the schooner was allowed to proceed without further molestation.

Sir Frederick Maitland thereupon moved to the anchorage of Lung-keet, upon which the Chinese Admiral, Kwan Tienpei, the potent and fear-inspiring, addressed a complaint to him against Captain Elliot for seeking to discontinue in his letters the words " humble address " *(pin)* and substituting " letters of intelligence " *(shusin)* instead, in disobedience of the regulations, and inquired the motives of the war vessels coming to the anchorage of Lung-keet. To this, Sir Frederick Maitland answered that he had come to demand explanations for an insult offered to the Sovereign of his country, in the person of himself, by firing at and boarding a British vessel under the pretext that he might be on board, and requesting that officers might be sent to him for explanations. On the next day, the 5th August, Chinese officers were sent on board the *Wellesley* and denied in writing any sanction being given by the Chinese Admiral to the firing on the *Bombay*. Sir Frederick Maitland informed the officers that the trade had ceased to be in the hands of the East India Company and was then under the direct control and protection of the British Sovereign : that frequent visits of British men-of-war must therefore be expected, because it was in accordance with the genius of the English Government to look after the interests of its subjects in foreign countries.

The next thing which happened,—shewing the temper of the Chinese authorities at this time,—was an attempt to execute a criminal in front of the European factories. This was prevented, but not without a riot—and the prisoner was then executed at one of the usual places appointed for the purpose. The offence for which the prisoner suffered the penalty of death was that of selling opium, and there is no doubt that the attempt to execute him in front of the factories was with the purpose of fixing upon the foreign community generally the seriousness of the Governor's orders to stop the opium trade.

During the whole of the year 1838, the opium trade was the subject of many reports by the local authorities to the Imperial Government, and a proposition, made by the Chinese merchants for legalising the import and sale of opium, was considered and ultimately rejected by the Imperial Council. Governor Tang then, in January, 1839, issued a proclamation, addressed to the foreign merchants, informing them that a land and marine preventive service had been established, that all foreign vessels engaged in the traffic would be driven forth, all boats and buildings used for opium would be taken, and all persons found selling or inhaling the drug would be seized and treated as criminals. He also announced that a Special Commissioner was hourly expected at Canton to carry out the orders of the Great Emperor, that his purpose was "to cut off " utterly the source of this noxious abuse, to strip bare and root " up this enormous evil : and, though his axe should break in " his hand or the boat should sink from beneath him, yet " will he not stay his efforts till the work of purification be " accomplished."

On the 26th February following, a Chinese, accused of dealing in opium, was suddenly brought down into the square before the foreign factories, accompanied by a considerable force of troops, and immediately put to death by strangulation. All the foreign flags were thereupon hauled down. Captain Elliot, who was at Macao at the time, at once came up to Canton and addressed a remonstrance to the Governor of Canton against this insult.

The High Commissioner Lin arrived at Canton in March, and addressed two edicts, one to the Hong merchants and the other to the foreigners of all nations, requiring all the opium in the store ships to be surrendered, and bonds to be given by the owners that they would never bring any more on penalty of death.

On the 21st of March, all foreigners were forbidden to go to Macao; communication with Whampoa was cut off, and the factories surrounded with armed men. Captain Elliot, who had gone to Macao, expecting—from the assembly of a considerable Chinese force in that neighbourhood and the collection of vessels, boats of war, and fire-ships under the forts at Bocca Tigris— that the High Commissioner would commence operations from Macao, at once returned to Canton, and passed through the cordon of armed boats, unarmed, and landed at the factories, to the great relief of the distressed English merchants there. Mr. Dent, one of the largest holders of opium, was summoned by the High Commissioner to attend his tribunal within the city. Captain Elliot communicated to the Chinese Government his readiness to let Mr. Dent go into the city with *him*, and upon the distinct written stipulation, under the High Commissioner's seal, that he was never to be removed for one moment out of his sight. The native servants were then taken away from all the English factories, supplies were cut off, and all the foreigners subjected to a close imprisonment.

On the 25th March, Captain Elliot demanded passports for all the English ships and people at Canton, and on the following day he received the commands of the High Commissioner Lin to deliver over all the opium in the possession of British subjects —20,283 chests—to be destroyed.

At six o'clock the following morning, Captain Elliot issued a public notice calling on all British subjects to surrender the whole of the opium in their possession into his hands to be delivered over to the Chinese Government, holding himself responsible on behalf of Her Majesty's Government.

This demand was at once answered by the delivery of all the receiving orders for 20,283¾ chests of opium, being all the opium on the receiving vessels at Lin Tin or near the coast outside. The Commissioner, however, would not relax his hold over the foreign community until he had the opium in his possession. On the 2nd of April, he therefore notified to Captain Elliot that the servants should be restored on the delivery of one fourth, the passage boats should be permitted to run on the delivery of one-half, the trade should be opened on the delivery of three-fourths, and, on the delivery of the whole, everything should go on as usual. In case of breach of faith, after three days, the supply of water should be cut off; after three days more, the supply of food should be stopped; and after three days more, the last degree of severity should be visited on Captain Elliot himself.

On the 5th April, Commissioner Lin required the owners of the opium to enter into a bond that they would not again introduce any opium into the inner land; that, if such be done, the vessel containing the opium and cargo should be confiscated to the use of the Government, and that the parties offending would readily submit to suffer death at the hands of the Celestial Court.

On the 10th of April, Commissioner Lin and the Governor of Canton proceeded to the Bogue to witness the delivery of the opium in person, but, owing to the tardiness of the receiving ships in coming to the Bogue, the whole of the opium was not delivered up until the 4th of May. On the following day the trade was reopened and affairs resumed their usual course.

The destruction of the opium, valued at six million dollars, commenced on the 3rd and was completed on the 23rd May— as many as 1,000 chests a day being destroyed. The work of destruction took place in the presence of Commisioner Lin himself, at Chinkow, near the Bogue forts, and about five miles from Chuenpee. The Chinese authorities were unwilling to cast the opium into the river lest the fish should be thereby poisoned. The method of destruction adopted was this :—three large vats or trenches, 100 feet long, 75 feet broad, and 7 feet deep, were constructed ; each trench was flagged with stone and lined round with heavy timbers, and was separately enclosed, having an entrance only on one side, which was carefully guarded day and night. The trenches were filled for about two feet deep with fresh water, into which the balls of opium, having previously been broken into pieces, were thrown. Coolies were employed in the trenches in keeping the opium turned up from the bottom of the vat, other coolies were employed in spreading salt and lime over the whole surface of each trench. When the whole was in a state of decomposition and in a sufficiently liquid state to be drawn off, a sluice, furnished with a screen to stop solid pieces, was opened and the liquid flowed into the creek.

The Europeans were detained at their factories in Canton until the 23rd May, the date of the completion of the delivery of the opium, and on the next day Captain Elliot, with most of the foreign merchants, retired from Canton to Macao.

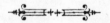

CHAPTER III.

HISTORY OF HONGKONG—*continued*.

Merchant Ships assemble in Hongkong Waters.—The First Criminal Trial.—
Movements of Commissioner Lin.—Exodus from Macao.—Arrival
of the British Expedition.—Blockade of the Canton River.—Capture
of Chusan Island.—Blockade of the Coast.—Negotiation with
Keshen.—Capture of the Bogue Forts.—The Chuenpee Treaty and
Cession of the Island of Hongkong.

AFTER the serious events which had happened at Canton,
ending with the destruction of the opium, Captain
Elliot was persuaded that neither Englishmen nor
English ships would ever be safe again within the limits of the
port of Canton until the whole intercourse between England and
China was placed upon an entirely different footing. He
therefore determined to keep the British shipping entirely outside
of the Bocca Tigris, much to the disgust of Commissioner Lin,
who was anxious to report to the Throne the peaceful resumption
of the British trade, and dared not venture to leave the provinces
until he could do so.

A large number of ships then collected in the waters of
Hongkong, nearly fifty of them carrying the British flag. The
seamen could not, of course, be prevented from landing, with the
result that, on the 7th July, a riot took place in one of the villages,
in which several sailors of the ships *Carnatic* and *Mangalore* were
engaged, and a native lost his life. The situation of the English
people in China became at once most critical. The High
Commissioner insisted upon the delivery of a man to him for

execution. Captain Elliot came to Hongkong with the view of settling matters satisfactorily, set in motion his criminal jurisdiction, and placed six men on trial on board the ship *Fort William*. The trial took place on the 12th and 13th August, when two men were found guilty of riot only and sentenced to three months hard labour in England and a fine of £15: and three men were found guilty of riot and assault and sentenced to six months like imprisonment in England and a fine of £25. This is the first occasion of the exercise of English criminal jurisdiction in China.

These proceedings did not satisfy Commissioner Lin, who moved down to Heung Shan, 40 miles from Macao, with 2,000 troops, stopped the supplies of food to British subjects, took away their servants, and threatened the inhabitants of Macao with a stoppage of their own supplies if they continued to assist the English. The Governor of Macao declared his inability to afford British subjects further protection after noon of the 26th August, at which hour they were all to embark in a body in the Governor's presence, with the troops under arms. Accordingly, all British subjects, with the whole fleet of British ships and boats, and every British flag, at the appointed hour set sail, in company, for Hongkong, where they arrived under the complete conviction that such a course was necessary for the general safety.

Her Majesty's ship *Volage*, Captain Smith, arrived early in September, and between that date and November, endeavoured to make arrangements with the Chinese authorities for the loading and unloading of British ships in the outer waters at Chuenpee. On November 3rd, while Captain Elliot was at Chuenpee, on board the *Volage*, for the purpose of making arrangements for bringing up the ships from Hongkong to Chuenpee, a Chinese squadron of twenty-nine sail, under the command of the Admiral, which had collected under the batteries, began to break ground, and, as the subsequent movements of this squadron were palpably hostile, Captain Smith took precautions to prevent the junks and fire-boats from passing inside his position during the night, with the result that a serious action at once commenced in which the Chinese squadron was dispersed by the *Volage* and her companion frigate the *Hyacinth*, and some of the junks destroyed. The Chinese soon, however, began to block up the passages leading from Hongkong to the Canton river, with the intention of destroying the merchant ships by fire-ships. This proceeding induced Captain Elliot to take measures to move the ships from Hongkong to Tonkoo bay, 20 miles nearer to Macao, which was done, much to the regret of the merchants, who preferred the waters of Hongkong.

At the commencement of the year 1840, the position of the English in China was very unsatisfactory and humiliating. Captain Elliot requested, in the name of Her Majesty, the permission of the Governor of Macao to land some merchandise into warehouses at Macao, upon paying the duties ; but even this request was refused, such was the fear of the Portuguese of the Chinese, who had threatened to stop supplies if they in any way assisted the English. On the 14th January, an edict was received from the Emperor ordering foreigners of other nations to be submissive, but if they sheltered or protected the English, or conveyed them or their property into Chinese harbours, their punishment would be great.

The day of retribution, however, was fast approaching. The English Government had arranged with the East India Company that the latter should send out an expedition at the sole cost of the Imperial Government.

The expedition arrived at the end of June, and consisted of fifteen ships of war, four steamers, twenty-five transports, and about 4,000 land forces, under the command of Sir J. Gordon Bremer.

Captain Elliot at once issued a public notice to the Chinese that the Queen of England had appointed high officers to make known the true state of affairs to the Emperor of China, and Sir J. Gordon Bremer gave public notice of the blockade of the Canton river. The objects of the expedition were to obtain the recognition of the Queen of England as the independent sovereign of a civilized country; an apology for the treatment of Lord Napier; compensation for the losses caused to British merchants by the stoppage of the trade while Lord Napier was at Canton, and afterwards; and various regulations to provide for future security.

Every means failed to arrange matters with the Chinese authorities, and there was no alternative but to commence hostilities, to awaken the Emperor and his ministers to a sense of justice.

Having established the blockade of the Canton river, Sir J. Gordon Bremer sailed North, and when off Amoy, the *Blonde*, Captain Bourchier, was sent to the harbour with a letter to the Chinese Admiral stationed there, with the only result that no one could be found who would receive the letter. On the 2nd July, the Chinese, notwithstanding the white flag of the frigate, made a wanton attack on the defenceless boat—which was a second time sent off with the letter—with the endeavour to capture or destroy it. Captain Bourchier, seeing this, directed the guns of the *Blonde* upon the war-junks and batteries for nearly two hours, with terrific effect. This was done to impress upon the people that the quarrel was not with them—as Amoy itself could have been destroyed—but with their rulers alone.

Sir Gordon Bremer then proceeded, on board the *Wellesley*, to Tinghai, the capital of the island of Chusan, and demanded the surrender of the town within six hours. On Sunday morning, the 5th July, it was observed the Chinese were making vigorous efforts in erecting defensive works, and a message was sent by Sir Gordon Bremer to the Governor that a gun would be fired from the *Wellesley* at two o'clock in the afternoon, and, if replied to, that would be the signal for further hostilities. At half-past two the *Wellesley* fired a gun, which was returned by the guns from the town and the whole of the war-junks. The British men-of-war opened their broadsides upon the town and made sad havoc in a very short time. The Madras artillery landed and in two hours had placed four guns commanding the town, and the British flag was hoisted under a salute. The Chinese kept firing at intervals until ten o'clock at night, and to stop this a few shells were thrown into the city, one of which killed the civil magistrate. The Governor, finding further defence hopeless, drowned himself under the pretence of taking a bath.

Admiral Elliot arrived at Chusan on the 7th July, and at once placed a close blockade on the harbour of Ningpo, a city on the mainland opposite the island of Chusan. All efforts failed to send Lord Palmerston's letter to Peking, and the whole coast from Ningpo to the mouth of the Yang-tze-kiang was therefore blockaded by the British vessels. At the end of July, no further progress having been made, the British Admiral proceeded northward with a large fleet, and on August the 15th the chief portion of the squadron arrived at the mouth of the Peiho, within one hundred miles of the Imperial residence. Here Keshen, the Governor of the province and the third member of the Emperor's cabinet, received Lord Palmerston's letter without any difficulty, and directed the ships to be supplied with provisions, cattle, &c., without payment in return. He also asked for ten days to communicate to Peking and receive an answer, which was granted. On the 28th August, and following day, a conference was held on shore, between Captain Elliot and Keshen, without any satisfactory result, further time being required to communicate with Peking. Ultimately Captain Elliot allowed the conference to be adjourned to Canton, Keshen having considered that the difficulties could be better arranged at the spot where the troubles commenced.

The Emperor recalled the High Commissioner Lin from Canton, the edict of recall stating that so far from having been of any help in the affair, he (Lin) had caused the waves of confusion to arise, and a thousand disorders were sprouting ; that it appeared he was no better than a wooden image. He was also ordered, with the speed of flames to Peking, for examination. Keshen was appointed the new Commissioner. The adjournment of the conference to Canton was simply a device of Keshen to gain time and to wear out the British soldiers.

On the 6th January, 1841, a proclamation was received from the Emperor which terminated all hopes of any amicable arrangements being made. This proclamation directed the Chinese authorities to utterly reject any petitions presented by foreigners, and that if any of their ships sailed near the ports on the coast, the matchlocks and artillery were at once to be opened "and the thundering attack be made dreadful." On January 9th, the British authorities determined to attack the Bogue forts in the Canton river. The squadron was anchored about three miles below the first forts. The steamers *Nemesis, Enterprise,* and *Madagascar,* were first employed in conveying ashore the land forces, consisting of a battalion of royal marines, a detachment of royal artillery, with one twenty-four pounder howitzer, and two six-pounder field-pieces, as well as detachments of the 26th, 49th, and 37th Madras native infantry, and a detachment of Bengal volunteers. The whole force, amounting to 1,400, were under the command of Major Pratt, of the 26th or Cameronian regiment. The royal artillery guns were dragged through a winding valley for two miles, and placed where there was a clear view of the Chinese force. The *Queen* and *Nemesis* were stationed so as to throw shells into the hill-forts and the entrenchments on the inner side. The *Calliope*, *Hyacinth*, and *Lorne*, under the command of Captain (afterwards Sir Thomas) Herbert, were told off to bombard the lower fort on Chuenpee. The *Wellesley* with the other large vessels, the *Samarang*, *Modeste*, *Druid* and *Columbine*, took up a position further up the river.

As soon as the Chinese saw the land forces approaching, they waved their flags in defiance and opened fire from their field batteries, which was quickly returned by the British artillery. The *Queen*, with her sixty-eight pounder, and the *Nemesis*, with her thirty-two pounder, at the same time shelled the hill-fort. The Chinese could not long withstand the heavy fire, and in less than half an hour the entrenchments were carried, the hill-fort captured, and the British flag hoisted on its summit. During this time, the lower fort had been silenced by the three ships placed before it. The Chinese left the battery and retreated towards a wooded hill, which was already occupied by the royal marines and the 37th native infantry. The enemy was soon overcome, but the havoc was dreadful ; only about a hundred of the Chinese troops accepted quarter.

The fort of Taikok, on the opposite side to Chuenpee, was simultaneously attacked and carried ; a breach was made in the solid masonry by the broadsides from the *Druid*, and the guns of the fort were silenced. The seamen and marines were then landed and carried the fort by storm. The steamers then moved into Anson's bay, where the Chinese war-junks were assembled, and destroyed eleven of them, the first Congreve-rocket from the *Nemesis* taking immense effect in blowing up one of the largest war-junks with all her crew. The Chinese loss in killed and wounded could not be ascertained, but it is stated 500 were killed. The British forces did not lose one man.

The forces then prepared to advance to attack the forts at the Bogue, when Admiral Kwan sent a flag of truce with a chop to Captain Elliot, requesting three days' grace to enable him to communicate with Keshen, which Captain Elliot granted.

The result of this armistice was the preliminary treaty of Chuenpee, dated 19th January, 1841, between Her Majesty's plenipotentiary, Captain Elliot, and the Imperial Commissioner Keshan, involving (1) the cession of the island and harbour of Hongkong to the British Crown; (2) an indemnity to the British Government of six millions of dollars; (3) direct official intercourse between the two countries upon an equal footing; and (4) the trade of the port of Canton to be opened within ten days after the Chinese New Year.

On the 25th January, Sir Edward Belcher and some other officers from H.M.S. *Sulphur* landed on the island of Hongkong, at Possession Point, and Her Majesty's health was drunk, with three cheers, on Possession Mount. The next day, the 26th, the squadron arrived; the Union Jack was hoisted on Possession Mount, and formal possession taken of the Island by Commodore Sir J. Gordon Bremer, under a *feu-de-joi* from the marines and the Royal Salute from the ships-of-war.

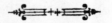

CHAPTER IV.

HISTORY OF HONGKONG—*continued*.

Captain Elliot assumes the Government of Hongkong.—Refusal of the
Emperor of China to ratify the Treaty of Chuenpee.—Punishment
and Death of Keshen and Admiral Kwan.—Resumption of Hostilities.—Capture of the Bogue Forts.—Destruction of the Defences
of Canton.—Armistice of Commissioner Yang—Chinese Plot for
Destruction of the British Forces.—Arrival of Lord Gough.—
Capture of Canton and Ransom of the City.—Arrival of Sir Henry
Pottinger.—The China War.—The First Treaty with China.—Cession
of Hongkong ratified.

APTAIN Elliot, as Her Majesty's Chief Superintendent
of Trade, assumed the Government of the island of
Hongkong, and by proclamation, dated the 30th
January, 1841, by Captain Elliot, as Her Majesty's plenipotentiary,
and Sir J. Gordon Bremer, as Commander in Chief, it was
announced that all native persons residing in Hongkong were then
subjects of the Queen of England, that they should be protected
against all enemies whatsoever, and secured in the free exercise
of their religious rites, ceremonies, and social customs, and in the
enjoyment of their lawful private property and interests; that
they would be governed, pending Her Majesty's further pleasure,
according to the laws, customs, and usages of the Chinese—every
description of torture excepted—by the elders of the villages,
subject to the control of a British Magistrate; and that Chinese
ships and merchants, resorting to the port of Hongkong for
purposes of trade, were thereby exempted from charges or duties
of any kind to the British Government. Whether Hongkong was
to become a permanent British possession remained, however, an
unsettled question for many months.

The Emperor of China not only refused to ratify the proceedings of Keshen in ceding the island of Hongkong, but, on the contrary, on the 27th January, an imperial edict was issued stating that "A report has been received from Keshen setting forth the attack on and capture of certain ports by the English. The rebellious disposition of these foreigners being plainly manifest, there remains no other course but to destroy and wash them clean away and thus display the majesty of the empire." Troops were also ordered to proceed to Canton from different parts of the empire.

Keshen, once the Prime Minister of China, was sent in chains from Canton to Peking, where he was imprisoned and left to starve for a time. He was then ordered to be cut in small pieces for the fowls of the air and his property was declared confiscated. Kwan, the naval commander, was degraded for having shewn himself devoid of talent; his button and insignia of rank were taken from him, but he was allowed to "labour to attain merit, and shew forth his after endeavours." Admiral Kwan was, however, killed on board of his own vessel, and was, in the Chinese language, reported to have died "leaning gracefully against the mast."

The time for the ratification of the treaty with Keshen expired on the 25th February, but, it being well known to the British authorities that the Chinese would act on the Emperor's instructions, that day was occupied in preparing for the coming struggle and arranging for the capture of the Bogue forts. Men were landed, with three howitzers, on South Wangtung, and at daylight the next morning, the 26th, they opened fire upon the Chinese fortifications on the northern island. The *Queen* steamer, *Blenheim* and *Melville* commenced to attack the forts at eleven o'clock a.m., and the Chinese instantly returned the fire from the sand batteries they had lately erected near Anson's Bay. After

a few broadsides the enemy fled up the hill. Sir J. Le Senhouse
then landed with about 300 men and carried all before them.
The British flag was flying on the batteries shortly after one
o'clock p.m. At the same time the *Calliope* was engaged on
the western side of Wangtung ; the advanced squadron, consisting
of the *Samarang, Herald,* and *Alligator,* took up their position
on the north side of the island ; while the *Wellesley, Druid,* and
Modeste attacked the western defences.

The Chinese fire ceased about twelve o'clock, upon which
Major Pratt landed, with detachments of the 26th and 49th,
followed by the marines under Captain Ellis, and the 37th
Marine Native Infantry under Captains Duff and Mee.

The next day the advanced squadron, under the command
of Captain Herbert, routed a Chinese force of upwards of 2,000
troops of élite, who were strongly entrenched on the left bank of
the river, and defended by upwards of 100 pieces of artillery.
The Chinese made an obstinate resistance, but were eventually
routed with great loss. The casualties on the side of the
British forces were reported as inconsiderable.

The Emperor was furious on hearing of the fall of the forts,
and ordered Keshen to be brought to Peking and the rebellious
minister and his whole family to be put to death on the very
day of his arrival.

On the 3rd March, 1841, the Chinese resumed hostilities
from a masked battery constructed at the north-east end of
Whampoa; the battery was soon captured and twenty guns
destroyed. On the 7th the works in advance of Howqua's fort
were occupied, and on the 13th the Chinese fort at the Macao
passage, Canton, was taken by Captain Herbert. Captain Hall,
of the *Nemesis,* proceeded with his ship and the boats of the
Samarang and *Atalanta* from Macao to Canton by the inner
passage, and, with his small force, captured and destroyed seven

C

small batteries, with 105 pieces of cannon, as well as nine war
junks. On the 19th the remaining defences of Canton, in the
Macao passage, and at the Dutch folly, were taken and destroyed,
together with a large number of war-junks, whilst the foreign
factories were occupied by the British troops and the city of
Canton placed under the guns of the squadron. An armistice was
then agreed upon between the High Commissioner Yang (who
had succeeded Keshen) and Captain Elliot, part of the terms
of which were that the port of Canton was to be open to the
ships of all nations, and that the ships of war were to remain
near the neighbourhood of the English factories.

Things apparently went smoothly from this date to the
middle of May ; every facility was given to British commerce, and
friendly intercourse had taken place between Captain Elliot and
the four new commissioners who had been sent to Canton, as it
was believed, to arrange the demands of the British Government.
During this time, however, the Chinese had been very busy in
completing and manning numerous batteries along the banks of
the river, strange soldiers had also arrived in great numbers, and
on the 21st May, Captain Elliot had satisfied himself that a
Chinese plot was about to be carried out for the destruction of
the British forces and merchants. At Captain Elliot's recommendation, all British merchants left Canton that day. The
Chinese commenced the attack the same night, at about ten
o'clock, by sending fire-rafts against the British vessels, and
this they continued to do the whole night. The fire-rafts were
destroyed by the *Nemesis*, *Modeste*, *Pylades*, and *Algerin*, before
they did any damage, and at daylight the ships moved towards
the western fort at Shameen, which had opened fire, and silenced
it in a few minutes. The *Nemesis* also attacked a flotilla of war-
junks, sinking thirty-nine, with an equal number of fire-boats and
fishing junks. During this time 2,000 Chinese troops, sent by

the Chinese Commander, Yihshan, ransacked the British factories for arms—indiscriminate plunder ensued, and every particle of property was carried away. On the 25th May the British forces, under the command of Sir Hugh (afterwards Lord) Gough, arrived in the Macao passage, and the same day a detachment of the 49th occupied a fortress on the top of a hill eastward of the forts, while the 18th and 49th, under Major-General Burrell, attacked a village, close to the suburbs, filled with about 4,000 Chinese troops, which they soon cleared. The next day the Canton authorities sent a Mandarin to propose terms of peace, and a truce was arranged with Captain Elliot, part of the terms being that the Tartar troops should retire to a distance of sixty miles, and a ransom of $500,000 be paid for the city. The Tartar troops left accordingly, but, on the 29th, General Gough discovered large bodies of troops on the heights above Canton, about three miles to the rear of his head-quarters. Thinking this a ruse, General Gough provided for a strick watch to be kept over the city and then attacked the heights. The Chinese troops were totally routed with the loss of 1,500 killed and 5,000 wounded. The loss to the British troops was 14 killed and 120 wounded, but they also suffered severely from the great heat.

On the 31st May, the Canton authorities paid the sum of $500,000, and the troops returned from the heights to their ships. These events, however, did not succeed in obtaining the ratification by the Chinese Government of the cession of Hongkong, and it was not until the 29th August, 1842, that the treaty of Nanking was entered into, under which the Emperor of China ceded to Her Majesty the Queen of Great Britain the island of Hongkong in perpetuity.

Sir Henry Pottinger arrived at Hongkong on the 10th August, 1841, as sole plenipotentiary and minister to the Court of

Peking, but remained only twenty-four hours, and then proceeded North. On the 26th of August, he announced the capture of Amoy, after a short defence, and, on the 2nd October following, the recapture of Tinghai, the capital of the Chusan group. The city of Chinhae, the key to Ningpo, yielded to the spirited attack of the British forces on the 10th October, and the city of Ningpo was occupied with little resistance three days after.

The British troops and fleet wintered at Ningpo and Chusan, and, although the Chinese had been making preparations with great vigor all over the empire for the extermination of the "barbarians," nothing serious occurred until the 10th March, 1842, when the Chinese troops, to the number of about 12,000, attempted to retake Ningpo, but were repulsed with great slaughter. The Chinese also made an attempt to retake Chinhae, but were quickly repulsed. On May the 21st, Admiral Parker announced the capture of Chapu. The *Cornwallis*, *Blonde*, and *Modeste*, by the exertions of Commanders Kellett and Collinson in surveying and sounding, were enabled to take up a good position against the sea batteries, and did effective work in destroying the batteries,—as well as a gun foundry, gunpowder manufactory, extensive arsenals, and great quantities of gingals, matchlocks, bows, and arrows. The city of Shanghai was captured on the 19th June, and on the 20th July, the whole British force, amounting to seventy sail of vessels, had advanced up the Yangtzekiang and anchored abreast the city of Chinkiang, This city is over four miles in circumference and the works of defence were admirably constructed, so that nothing but cannon could have made any impression upon them. The Tartar troops, amounting to 3,000 men, opened a heavy and incessant fire of cannon, gingals, wall-pieces and matchlocks, and it was not until late in the evening before the enemy disappeared, after the loss of about one-third of their number. The Tartar general, seeing the city taken, retired to his house, made his servants set fire to it, and sat in his chair till he was burned to death.

The city of Chinkiang is situated at the junction of the grand canal with the Yangtszkiang, and its position—commanding the interior route from South China to the capital—was of great importance from a military point of view. Arrangements were therefore made for placing a strong British garrison at this city, and the remainder of the expedition sailed for Nanking, forty miles distant up the river.

On the 11th August everything was ready for the attack, when the Chinese displayed a white flag. Several conferences then ensued, and on the 29th, a treaty of peace was arranged between Sir Henry Pottinger and the High Commissioners, Kiying and Ilipu. The terms of peace included the cession of the Island of Hongkong "to be possessed in perpetuity by Her Britannic Majesty, her heirs and successors, and to be governed by such laws as Her Majesty the Queen of Great Britain shall see fit to direct." British subjects, with their families and establishments, were also to be allowed to reside—for the purpose of carrying on their mercantile pursuits without molestation or restraint—at the cities and towns of Canton, Amoy, Foochow-foo, Ningpo and Shanghai, and the Emperor of China agreed to pay the sum of six millions of dollars as the value of the opium delivered up at Canton in the month of March, 1839, as a ransom for the lives of Her Britannic Majesty's Superintendent and subjects who had been imprisoned and threatened with death by the Chinese high officers. His Imperial Majesty further agreed to pay, to the British government, the sum of three millions of dollars, on account of debts due to British subjects by some of the co-hong who had become insolvent, and the further sum of twelve millions of dollars for the expenses of the British expedition.

When the terms of peace had been read, Ilipu, the senior Commissioner, paused as if expecting something more, and then asked "is that all?" Mr. Morrison, who acted as interpreter, inquired of Lieutenant-colonel Malcolm if there were anything else, and received an answer in the negative, whereupon Ilipu immediately stated "all shall be granted—it is settled—it is finished" and with great tact closed the negotiations. The treaty was approved and ratified by the Emperor of China on the 24th day of the 9th Month in the 22nd year of his reign (October 27th, 1842), and by Her Majesty, and the Great Seal affixed on the 31st December, 1842. The ratifications were exchanged at Hongkong, June 26th, 1843.

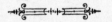

CHAPTER V.

HISTORY OF HONGKONG—*continued*.

Hongkong becomes a permanent British Possession.—First Land Sale.—
Recall of Captain Elliot.—Hongkong declared a Free Port.—The
Charter of the Colony.—Increase and Character of the Population.—
Commercial Progress.—Revenue and Expenditure.

LL doubts as to the island of Hongkong being selected
as a permanent British colony disappeared on the
conclusion of the Treaty of Nanking in August,
1842. In the draft of the Treaty, a blank had been left for the
name of the island to be ceded for a British port, and the island
of Chusan was strongly urged in some quarters as the most
suitable for the purpose. But between the preliminary treaty of
Chuenpee in January, 1841, and the arrival of Sir Henry
Pottinger in the following August, British trade had already
commenced to establish itself at Hongkong, and month by month
the trade increased and the magnificent harbour of Hongkong
began to be more appreciated as the best anchorage for ships in
the stormy China seas. The name of Hongkong was therefore
inserted in the blank space in the Treaty and Hongkong became
thenceforth a permanent British possession, the possession of
which dated back to January, 1841.

Captain Charles Elliot, R.N., was the first Chief Superintendent
of Trade and ex-officio Governor of the island, but did not long
enjoy that position. In June, 1841, Mr. A. R. Johnston, as

Deputy Superintendent, became also ex-officio Governor during the absence of Captain Elliot. On the 14th June, 1841, the first sale of land, consisting of 51 lots with sea frontages, took place by auction, the biddings being at an annual rent without premium. The upset price was at the rate of $600 an acre per annum, but some of the lots realized at the rate of $2,400 an acre per annum. In July, 1841, despatches were received from the Secretary of State disapproving of the Chuenpee treaty and recalling Captain Elliot, and on the arrival of Sir Henry Pottinger, as Governor, in the following month, he directed all sales of land to be stopped until Her Majesty's Government had decided on the question of the tenure upon which lands should be granted.

On the 6th February, 1842, Hongkong was declared a free port, by Sir Henry Pottinger, and the construction of roads through the island was commenced. The island and its dependencies were erected into "the Colony of Hongkong" by Royal Letters Patent, bearing date the 5th April, 1843. These Letters Patent constituted the original Charter of the Colony, and provided for the Government of the Colony by the Governor and Executive and Legislative Councils, and remained in force until the 19th January, 1888, when they were revoked by new Letters Patent of that date which are still in force.

The history of Hongkong from 1843 is a history of rapid and almost unexampled progress in population, commerce, buildings, and public works.

When the island of Hongkong was first taken possession of, in 1841, the inhabitants numbered about 4,000 and consisted only of native fishermen and agricultural labourers, living in a few villages and hamlets; and the promontory of Kowloon contained a native population of about 800. In the year 1842 the population had increased to 23,000. In 1861, nineteen years later, the population was returned at 119,321; in 1871, at *124,198;*

in 1881, at 160,402; and in 1891, at 221,141. The census of
1891 gives the following particulars:—

Europeans and Americans	8,545
Other nationalities	1,901
Chinese	210,995
Total	221,441

The annual increase in the population is at the rate of 3 per
cent and has kept on steadily at that average rate for the last 30
or 40 years and is now therefore increasing to the extent of about
7,000 per annum.

It will thus be seen that, within a little over 50 years of its
existence, Hongkong has risen from a comparatively barren and
uninhabited island to the rank of one of the smaller capital cities
of the world, and that this has arisen solely from the necessities
of British commerce with China and the indomitable energy
and perseverance of the merchants who first utilised the harbour
of Hongkong as a British Port.

The Europeans and Americans are mostly temporary residents.
They come to Hongkong to fulfil their mission as bankers,
merchants, professional men, or their assistants, &c. with the
intention of retiring from the Colony at the first convenient
opportunity. As the Colony advances, however, and home life
becomes more comfortable for Europeans, the numbers of those
who come to it to make it their home are constantly increasing.
In the early days of the Colony, Chinese robbers, smugglers, and
pirates in numbers made the island of Hongkong their chief
place of residence. Daring robberies at night were so frequent
that, as early as the year 1843, an Ordinance was passed forbidding
the natives to be out of doors after nightfall without a lantern
and pass. Robberies then became frequent in the daytime. As

an instance of those daylight robberies—even so late as the year 1867—the experience of Mr. Cuthbert Collingwood, related in his "Rambles of a Naturalist," may be quoted:—He had walked down the Queen's Road, the main street of Victoria, Hongkong, and, intending to make a slight *détour*, turned into a street leading up the hill. It was just mid-day, and the streets through which he was walking were thronged with people, either passing to and fro, or standing at the doors of their houses, or looking from their windows; but they were all, without exception, Chinese. Having gone a short distance up the street in question, he crossed into a parallel street, intending to descend into the Queen's Road again, and was so descending when, as he narrated—"I found myself suddenly in the midst of a knot of some eight or ten Chinamen. There was nothing in their dress or appearance which directed my attention to the probability that their object was robbery or outrage; and I was just passing on, when they made a simultaneous rush upon me and pushed me down, one of them striking me in the face, but so suddenly and unexpectedly that I had not a moment's opportunity for defence. While several pinioned me on the ground, one unbuttoned my coat and detached my gold watch and chain, upon which they all made off, leaving me to gather myself up as I best could." Of course the robbers escaped, particularly as it is almost impossible for a stranger to distinguish one Chinaman from another—such is their apparent similarity that they defy detection.

In those days robberies with violence in the streets of Victoria, and piracies in the waters near to Hongkong, were common. It was unsafe to walk alone in the suburbs—and it was unsafe to go almost anywhere after dark without taking due precautions.

The boat population of the Colony, who live in their floating dwellings, numbers 32,035. This population is now a very orderly one compared with two generations ago, when they were generally considered as Chinese pirates, and for Europeans to travel by Chinese fast boats was a great risk. The tragical death in 1854 of Mr. George Perkins, a retired partner of the house of Messrs. Russell and Company, as narrated by W. R. B. Forbes in his Personal Reminiscences, is a painful instance of the murderous nature of the Chinese boat-people in those days. Mr. Perkins had been on a visit to the United States, and was returning to Macao, where he had his residence, viâ San Francisco and the Sandwich Islands, in the Hamburg barque *Concordia*, bound for Hongkong. The barque left the Islands in March, 1854, and on arrival in Green Island passage, making for Hongkong harbour, a Chinese boat being within hail, Mr. Perkins bargained with the captain of the boat to be carried over to Macao, partly because of a dislike to Hongkong, and partly to show his indifference to the supposed danger of falling in with Chinese pirates. Mr. Perkins never arrived at Macao, and after a great search for the boat and crew, they were found, ánd the crew—consisting of the Captain, his wife, and two or three Chinese boys—brought to trial in Hongkong. One of the boys turned Queen's evidence, and it was ascertained that Mr. Perkins was murdered the same afternoon that he engaged the boat. He was asleep at the time, his throat being cut as he lay upon his back. He had taken his trunks into the boat, but no money nor valuables. A few small articles were found, but no trace of his remains or of the trunks.

The method of attack and capture adopted by Chinese pirates in former days, when sailing ships were frequent, was to drop down in their junks in couples—held together by a cable—upon the bows of an unsuspecting ship, and so bring them, with their hordes of savages, close alongside, when, with their long poles and hooks, they would swarm on deck and, by force of numbers, soon effect a capture. In these days, and since steamers have become too numerous to render the old system of attack safe and profitable, the methods adopted by the pirates are to embark as passengers on board the steamer intended to be attacked, and, at a convenient opportunity, the captain is shot and any others who show resistance—the rest of the crew and passengers are imprisoned while the steamer is looted and the loot placed in junks, which are waiting at the selected spot of attack. The most notable and tragic of these attacks by pirates were those on board the steamer *Spark*, between Hongkong and Macao, in 1874; the steamer *Greyhound*, a short distance from Hongkong, in 1884; and the steamer *Namoa* 50 miles from Hongkong, in 1891—referred to subsequently in the events of the Colony. Piracy is little heard of now on the eastern coast of China, and is rapidly disappearing from the waters of southern China, in face of the precautions now taken in Hongkong in the embarkation of Chinese armed passengers.

The commerce of the Colony has progressed with the rapidity of the increase of the population. There have been years of depression and years of elevation—and always will be. but the average increase still goes on. The shipping frequenting the harbour has not been inaptly termed the "life blood of the Colony." In the year 1847, the number of ships which arrived in Hongkong (exclusive of Chinese vessels) was 694, of 229,465 tons : and of these only 163 imported and 193 exported merchandise into and from the Colony. These vessels were square-rigged and traded for the most part between India and China. The following statement shews the number and tonnage of vessels entered and cleared in Hongkong for the years 1861, 1871, 1881 and 1891, which gives at a glance the increase in each decade for that period :—

Vessels Cleared.

YEAR.	NUMBER.	TONNAGE.
1861...	1,259	658,196
1871...	34,550	3,360,622
1881...	27,553	4,533,304
1891...	27,157	6,773,243

Vessels Entered.

YEAR.	NUMBER.	TONNAGE.
1861...	1,286	652,187
1871...	28,635	3,158,519
1881...	27,051	4,475,820
1891...	26,953	6,768,918

The proportion of tonnage is, on an average, 53 per cent British, 31 per cent Chinese, and 16 per cent all other nations.

Hongkong is a free port and no exact statistics of its trade are available. A large quantity of goods imported are naturally consumed in the Colony—the import of vegetables alone amounting to about 80 tons a day. The number of junks entering the port of Victoria, engaged in the local trade, is upwards of 4,000 per annum, and the boats plying for hire within the waters of the Colony number 1,500. The number of steam launches in the harbour is over 100, and 75 are licensed to carry passengers.

The principal imports into the Colony are rice, flour, opium, tea, silk, oil, salt, iron, and other metals, cotton and woollen goods, and European and American manufactured articles of all descriptions; and the principal exports consist of sugar, tea, silk, &c. and the distribution of all imports. Granite, which, excepting vegetables, is about the only article the Colony produces, is also exported in considerable quantities to Macao and other places for building purposes.

The progress of the Colony is also strongly evidenced by its annual revenue. Hongkong is a free port, and no revenue is, therefore, derived from customs duties. The Colony is taxed under the heads of Licenses; Duties on Bank Notes; Stamp duties; and house tax on the annual values of all the occupied houses in the Colony, at the rate of 13 per cent for Victoria, $8\frac{3}{4}$ per cent for the Peak, and 7 per cent for Kowloon and the villages. There is also a fee on the tonnage of shipping of 2 cents per ton, of which 1 cent per ton is charged for the construction of the Gap Rock Lighthouse. There is also an opium monopoly, which brings a fair revenue to the Colony. In 1847 the revenue of the Colony was £31,078, but this revenue was not exceeded until the year 1855, when it amounted to £47,493, but fell the following year to £35,500, but increased again, in 1857, to £58,842; since which time to the present the revenue has appreciably increased every year, with little exception, until, in 1891, the revenue amounted to $2,025,302

The following shews the revenue and expenditure of the Colony for the years 1861, 1871, 1881 and 1891 :—

YEAR.	REVENUE.	EXPENDITURE.
1861...	$ 610,757	$ 526,274
1871...	$ 844,079	$ 896,040
1881...	$1,324,456	$ 981,582
1891...	$2,025,302	$2,449,086

The expenditure naturally exceeded the revenue for many years, and it was not until the year 1860 that the revenue overtook the expenditure. The most striking example of the increase in the resources of the Colony is shewn by the fact that the Colony now pays £40,000 a year to the Imperial Government by way of military contribution, or more than the whole of its annual revenue up to the year 1856.

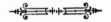

CHAPTER VI.

History of Hongkong—*Concluded.*

Administration of the Government.—Governors of Hongkong and Notable
Events in each Administration.

THE administration of the Government of the Colony
is in the hands of the Governor, with an Executive
Council of six Official Members, and a Legislative
Council of six Official and five Unofficial Members, presided over
by the Governor.   Three of the Unofficial Members are nominated
by the Crown, one being a Chinese, and the remaining two are
elected by local representative bodies, viz:—one by the Chamber
of Commerce, and one by the non-official Justices of the Peace.
The Unofficial Members are appointed for a period of six years.
The law of the Colony is the law of England as existed when
the Colony obtained a local legislature, that is, on the 5th April,
1843, except so far as the law should be inapplicable to the
local circumstances of the Colony or its inhabitants.   From the
commencement of the Colony, in 1841, to the 19th August, 1845,
the only Court was that held by the Chief Superintendent of Trade,
who had Criminal and Admiralty jurisdiction under the powers
conferred upon him under the original appointment of Chief
Superintendent in 1833.   A Supreme Court of Judicature was,
however, established in 1845 and reconstituted with two Judges
in 1873.

After the conclusion of the Treaty of Nanking, in August,
1842, Sir Henry Pottinger was made a G.C.B. and held the reins
as Governor of Hongkong and Chief Superintendent of Trade

until June, 1844, when he was succeeded by Mr. (afterwards Sir) John T. Davis. Under Sir Henry Pottinger's régime the Executive and Legislative Councils were established, and the departments of the public service organized. Major-General D'Aguilar was also appointed Lieutenant-Governor of the Colony. Sir Henry Pottinger created a great deal of dissatisfaction in the course adopted by him in reference to sales of land. He gave notice that no sale of land effected previous to the exchange of the Treaty ratifications would be recognized, and land was then offered for sale on leases for the short term of 75 years. Two newspapers, the *Eastern Globe* and the *Canton Register* (the latter previously published at Macao), were established in Hongkong during 1843. In this year also the London Missionary Society established themselves in the Colony, a Roman Catholic Church was opened, and a Mahometan mosque erected. Hongkong, however, began to have a bad name. The sanitary condition was reported as most alarming, and the bad character of the then native inhabitants and frequent robberies and murders contributed to increase the alarm. Sir Henry Pottinger expressed his determination to put down all pirates and smugglers, but without result. Howqua, the great Hong merchant, died in September 1843.

The administration of Sir John Davis dates from June, 1844, to the 30th March, 1848, and a review of his period of office seems to have been favourable on the whole. Great disputes took place between him and the community in respect to a registration ordinance passed on the 21st August, 1844, under which a charge was fixed for registering all Chinese residents on the Island.

The Chinese shewed their dislike to the ordinance by leaving in a body for the mainland. No food nor boats nor anything else could be obtained from them, until after the expiration of three days and the presentation of three memorials from the Colonists,

Sir John Davis cancelled the obnoxious ordinance. A bitter feeling was also created by the Government in the improper ejectment of holders of lots to make room for new improvements. The ordinance under which a Supreme Court of Judicature was established, was passed on the 21st August, 1844, to the great satisfaction of the inhabitants. Steps were also taken, during this year, for facilitating the postal arrangements and carriage of mails. The conveyance of a monthly mail from Gibraltar to Hongkong was inaugurated, in 1846, by the Spanish Government, but the rates charged were so excessive, that newspapers were practically excluded from the arrangement. The publication of the popular *Chinese Repository* was transferred to Hongkong in October, 1844, and the first number of the *China Mail* newspaper appeared on the 20th February, 1845.

Piracies and robberies were numerous during the administration of Sir John Davis. In March, 1846, a body of pirates, about eighty in number, landed and plundered the village of Shekpaiwan (now known as Aberdeen village) on the South side of the island, and in the following August a Government Notification advised residents to carry arms and not to proceed to any distance from the town alone, on account of the island being infested with robbers, and in March, 1847, an ordinance was passed for the prevention of piracy. The foundation stones of the Colonial Offices and the new church adjoining, now known as St. John's Cathedral, were laid in March, 1847. In January, 1848, General Stavely was appointed Lieut.-Governor of Hongkong, and Sir John Davis, having tendered his resignation as Governor, left for England on the 30th March, 1848, and Sir Samuel George Bonham (generally known as Sir George Bonham) was appointed his successor.

Sir George Bonham arrived in Hongkong on the 19th March, 1848, and administered the Government until April, 1854, with the exception of the greater part of the year 1852 during which he was absent in Europe and Major-General Jervois was acting Governor. There was little complaint made by the Colonists during the period of Sir George Bonham's administration, but crime, sickness, and natural calamities, were such as to cause grave anxiety all the time.

In July, 1848, a Chinese cook attempted to poison twenty-five soldiers of the Royal Artillery. In the following month some Chinese, condemned for piracy, received a free pardon, an act which called forth strong remonstrances from the Colonists. On the 31st August, 1848, a violent storm or typhoon swept over Hongkong, Macao and Canton. In Hongkong Harbour thirteen vessels were wrecked, many of the chief buildings were damaged, and several native houses destroyed; at Macao sixty-seven houses were destroyed and over a hundred Chinese killed, and the loss of life at Canton was also very great.

In November, 1848, a serious affray occurred in the harbour between the junkmen and the police, owing to the obscure wording of the regulations—two Chinese and one policemen were killed and many of the junkmen left the port. On the 1st March, 1849, Captain da Costa and Lieut. Dwyer, two officers of the Ceylon Rifles, were murdered near the village of Wongmakok, on the South side of the island, by a notorious pirate, named Chui Apo, who was subsequently sentenced to transportation for life, but hanged himself in the gaol.

On the 7th June, 1849, a curious affair happened at Macao. A religious festival was in progress and Mr. Summers, who was attached to the Prostestant Mission at Hongkong, and who was at Macao at the time, was imprisoned by the authorities for not taking off his hat on passing the Host. Captains Keppel and Troubridge, with some seamen from H.M.S. *Meander*, thereupon rescued Mr. Summers by force, a Portuguese soldier being unfortunately killed at the rescue.   On the 23rd August following, Governor Amaral, of Macao, was murdered by the Chinese.   Piracies were very numerous in the year 1849, but good service was done by a force under the command of Commander John D. Hay, R.N., an immense number of pirate junks being destroyed on the coasts adjacent to Hongkong and along the coasts of Cochin China.   During the month of June, 1850, Sir George Bonham, as Plenipotentiary, visited Shanghai, with the intention of proceeding to Tientsin on a diplomatic expedition in H.M.S. *Reynard*, but her draught prevented her crossing the bar at Taku, and, after handing in a letter to the authorities, she returned to Shanghai.   General Stavely left the Colony in February, 1851, for India, his departure being much regretted, and Major-General Jervois was appointed Lieutenant-Governor in the month of April following,   Mr. Gutzlaff, Chinese Secretary to the Superintendent of Trade, died on the 9th August, 1851.   The Oriental Bank was incorporated by Royal Charter in November 1851.   On the 28th December, 1851, one of the most serious conflagrations in the history of Hongkong happened.   As many as 472 Chinese houses were destroyed in the western part of the town and thirty lives lost.   Among the killed were Lieut.-Colonel Tomkyns and Lieutenant Lugg. Sir George Bonham left for Europe in April, 1852, and during his absence the government of the Colony was administered by Major-General Jervois.   In August, 1852, a murderous attack was made by two Chinese on the Rev. Mr. Van Genniss, a missionary at Shekpaiwan.   Piracies began to be numerous, nineteen cases were reported in Hongkong in 1852, increasing in 1853, to over seventy cases in the waters of Hongkong and the neighbourhood, and on the 5th August, 1853, a horrible tragedy was enacted on board the steamer *Arratoon Apcar*, the captain, officers, and passengers, to the number of twelve, being murdered by the Chinese crew. The number of burglaries and robberies from the person also rose to an extraordinary number in the year 1853

At this time the Chinese rebellion was making great progress. One of its effects was the rapid growth of the population of Hongkong, which had increased from 21,514 in 1848, to 39,017 in 1853, and when the rebels devastated the districts of the adjoining province of Kwantung, in the following year, the population of Hongkong rose suddenly to 55,715. No doubt a number of criminals from the mainland swelled this sudden increase, and to a large extent accounted for the extraordinary number of robberies happening at this period. During Sir George Bonham's administration, the opium question occasioned, for some time, serious discussions. The government of Sir Robert Peel had attempted to exclude opium from the trade of the Colony by permitting the Chinese government to impose a heavy tax upon the import of opium into China, with the only result that much harm was done to Hongkong merchants and the object of lessening its use among the Chinese could not be gained. The coolie traffic, as it was called, also created great interest and anxiety. A considerable trade had sprung up at Macao, in the year 1852, in the export of coolies to Peru. Hongkong, at first, shared in the trade, as most of the vessels employed were fitted up and provisioned in the Colony, but a series of mutinies occurring on those coolie ships, the true character of the trade was revealed as a veritable slave trade, and Hongkong withdrew from it entirely, and the merchants and traders devoted their attention to the development of the Chinese passenger trade with California, which, by the end of Sir George Bonham's term of office, had assumed enormous dimensions.

An important commercial event, during Sir George Bonham's administration, was the accomplishment of a fortnightly mail service between Europe and Hongkong, the contract for which was made with the P. & O. Steam Navigation Company, which company had previously run a monthly mail service since the year 1845. The new fortnightly service commenced in January 1853.

It was also during Sir George Bonham's term of administration that the Island of Hongkong was erected, by Letters Patent, dated 7th May, 1849, into a Bishop's See and diocese, called the Bishopric of Victoria, and the Reverend George Smith consecrated as the first Bishop of Victoria; and in 1850 an ordinance was passed, by the Legislative Council of the Colony, providing the Church, which was thenceforth designated the Cathedral Church of St. John.

Arrangements were also made, in the same year, for the formation of a botanical garden, which has since developed into the beautiful botanic gardens now existing.

Climatic sickness was so serious, during Sir George Bonham's administration, that Hongkong became proverbial for its supposed deadly climate. The worst years were 1848, 1850, 1851 and 1854, and the troops suffered most severely. It is pleasant, however, to record that the civilians assisted in every way they could to relieve the suffering soldiers. As a memento of the sickness, chiefly fever and dysentery, which swept over the troops in 1848, a handsome cup was, in February, 1849, presented to Messrs. Jardine, Matheson & Co., by the non-commissioned officers and men of the 95th Regiment, in gratitude for the kindness shown them by that firm during the heavy sickness which had visited the regiment.

Dr. (afterwards Sir John) Bowring, H. M. Consul at Canton, succeeded Sir George Bonham as Governor of Hongkong. He assumed his position of Governor on the 13th April, 1854, and administered the Government until May, 1859. In June, 1854, active measures were taken for the defence of the island, the news having arrived that war had been declared between England and Russia, and causing somewhat of a scare among the Colonists; and about the same time a panic was caused by a rumour, which was spread abroad, that an immense piratical fleet was about to attack Hongkong.

In 1856 hostilities had again broken out between England and China, owing to an insult to the British flag and the arrest, by the Chinese authorities, of some seamen on board the British lorcha *Arrow*, at Canton, on the 8th October, 1856, and an uneasy feeling began to prevail throughout the Colony in consequence. The Chinese authorities at Canton, in view of the impending hostilities, put a price upon the heads of foreigners and suggested the use of poison. In December, 1856, the steamer *Fei-ma* was attacked by pirates, but escaped, and although hulled in several places, none of her crew were hurt.

On the 13th January, 1857, the steamer *Thistle* was captured and burnt by mandarin soldiers disguised as passengers. Eleven Europeans and several Chinese were killed. Two days afterwards an attempt was made to poison the foreign residents in the Colony by means of arsenic placed in the dough of the principal baker in the Colony, named A-Lum, but the quantity used was so great that it caused vomiting to all who partook of the bread, and thus the lives of the intended victims were saved. The poisoners were never discovered. On the 23rd February the steamer *Queen* was also captured by Chinese soldiers who had embarked as passengers. The Captain and several Europeans were killed, and the vessel burnt. Incendiarism was at this time rampant among the natives and the loss to the Colony by conflagrations was considerable. In the month of March, 1857, following, the Chinese authorities took measures to stop all the native communication between Hongkong and Macao, and an edict was published ordering all Chinese to leave Hongkong, and in April the existence of a vast conspiracy was disclosed, organized at Canton, to carry on the war within the Colony by means of the piracies, murders, robberies, fires and poisonings which then afflicted the port.

On the 2nd July, 1857, Lord Elgin, Her Majesty's plenipotentiary to China, arrived at Hongkong, but left immediately afterwards for Calcutta in consequence of the outbreak of the Indian Mutiny. In September the Earl of Elgin returned to Hongkong, accompanied by Major-General Straubenzee and staff, and on the 28th December, following, the bombardment of Canton commenced; the capture was effected the next day, and the Viceroy Yeh was taken prisoner a few days afterwards. Lord Elgin then, in conjunction with Baron Gros, the French plenipotentiary, determined to proceed to Peking with an armed force, and reached the mouth of the Peiho river, which he found strongly defended by forts on both banks. The forts were taken by Admiral Sir M. Seymour, and the forces proceeded to Tientsin, where the plenipotentiaries were met by Chinese Commissioners to adjust the terms of a treaty. After much procrastination, as usual, by the Chinese Commissioners, under various pretexts, which were met by Lord Elgin with great determination, the Commissioners agreed to execute a treaty in the terms proposed to them by Lord Elgin and this was signed at Tientsin on the 26th June, 1858.

The treaty had no sooner been signed than a considerable exodus of the respectable Chinese in the Colony took place, owing to a proclamation issued by the Braves of the Kwangtung province ordering them to return home within a month, and threatening to punish their families left in their native towns and villages as rebels if they did not do so. The food supplies from the mainland were also stopped. In consequence of these acts and supported by resolutions passed at a public meeting held on the 29th July, 1858, the Governor issued a counter proclamation threatening the districts whence these threats issued with the retributive vengeance of the British Government unless the objectionable orders were withdrawn. H.M's gun-boat *Starling* was employed in the distribution of this proclamation and on her proceeding to the walled city of Namtow, on the Canton river, under a flag of truce, she was fired upon by the Imperial Chinese troops. General Straubenzee and Commodore the Honourable Keith Stewart, upon receiving intelligence of this insult, proceeded to the spot with a considerable military and naval force for the purpose of exacting retribution for the insult. Namtow was taken by assault, but not without loss—two military officers and three men being killed, and one naval officer and twelve men wounded. This action had the desired effect and the food supplies were sent to Hongkong as formerly.

Lord Elgin left Canton in March, 1859, and went direct to Singapore without calling at Hongkong! Mr. Bruce, H.M. Minister to Peking and Superintendent of British Trade in China, arrived in Hongkong, in April, 1859, *en route* for the North to exchange the ratifications of the treaty of Tientsin.

Sir John Bowring's administration made no apparent headway against the piracies which afflicted the Colony throughout the whole term of his administration. The pirates made Hongkong the centre of their operations, here they obtained accurate information of the movements of the men-of-war and of the police, and were enabled to dispose of their plunder, and this they did notwithstanding the activity of the naval authorities who were continually engaged in making raids against the fleets of piratical junks which infested the waters of the Colony and neighbouring bays. In August, 1855, H.M's. brig *Bittern* had a severe encounter with pirates at Shei-foo, in which twenty-three junks were destroyed and 1,200 pirates killed—nineteen of the crew of the *Bittern* were wounded and the Commander killed during this engagement. Notwithstanding the apparent success of this action, piracies kept on increasing in numbers, as many as sixty-one occuring within the waters of the Colony from November, 1856, to October, 1857. In July, 1857, a cargo of sugar taken by the pirates was traced to the shop of Ma-chow Wong, a notorious pirate-spy and informer. He was tried on the 2nd September following for confederating with pirates, found guilty and sentenced to fifteen years transportation. One of the witnesses for the prosecution was Eli M. Boggs, an American, who had been two months previously found guilty of piracy and sentenced to transportation for life. It was believed that the sentences passed upon these two men and the activity of the naval authorities in searching for and destroying pirate vessels would have put an end to the infliction, but piracies still continued to an alarming extent, and expeditions sailing in search of pirate fleets were not at all uncommon. In March, 1859, an expedition, under the command of Captain Colville of the *Niger* and consisting of that vessel and the gunboats *Janus* and *Clown*, discovered a large nest of pirates in the Broadway near Macao. The pirates showed fight and fired at the British vessels, but without effect, and this expedition succeeded in destroying twenty pirate junks, together with a number of fast boats and guns, while about two hundred of the pirates were killed.

Sir John Bowring departed in May, 1859, and the Government was administered from that date until the arrival of Governor Sir Hercules Robinson, in the month of September following, by Colonel Caine. It was during Colonel Caine's administration that the news arrived of the sudden attack by the Chinese on the British fleet and retreat of the latter at the mouth of the Peiho on the 25th June, 1859, while the plenipotentiaries were proceeding to Peking to exchange the ratified treaty of Tientsin. The news of the disaster, however, did not affect the position of the Colonists with the natives. The Cantonese appeared to receive the news with sorrow, and regretted the continuation of the war with China which was the natural result. Canton was still in possession of the allied British and French forces and Mr. (afterwards Sir) Harry Smith Parkes, then the British Commissioner at Canton, obtained, on behalf of the Government, from the Governor General of the Two Kwang, the grant of a lease in perpetuity of the Kowloon peninsula. On the 24th October, 1860, the convention of Peking was settled by Lord Elgin, with two Chinese plenipotentiaries, under which the Emperor of China ceded the Kowloon peninsula to the British crown to be held as a dependency of the Colony of Hongkong, and the lease to Sir Harry Parkes was declared cancelled.

The peace between Great Britain and China, restored by the Peking Convention, has never since been broken, and there is no probability that it will ever be broken again.

The cession of the Kowloon peninsula caused a very curious squabble between the Civil, Naval, and Military authorities. Sir Hercules Robinson, as the Governor of the Colony, desired that it should be laid out for building purposes for the extension of the commerce of the Colony; the military officer in command required the whole of the peninsula for barracks, parade grounds, and military purposes generally; and the naval authorities put in their claim to the Imperial Government for a considerable portion of the foreshore for a Naval Yard, coal stores and other purposes supposed to be wanted for Admiralty use. This squabble is not yet at rest after 30 years of possession.

Sir Hercules Robinson's administration lasted until his departure for Ceylon in March, 1865, between which date and the arrival of his successor, Sir Richard Graves MacDonnell, in 1866, the Government of the Colony was administered by

Mr. W. T. Mercer.   Mr. Mercer was also acting Governor during
the absence of Sir Hercules Robinson in England in the
years 1862 and 1863.   The period of Sir Hercules Robinson's
administration is remarkable for the extraordinary progress of
the Colony, notwithstanding the continuation of the war with
China during the first few years of the period.   The Post
Office, which had hitherto been carried on by the Imperial
Government, was, in 1859, transferred to the Local Government
as a separate department.   Sir Hercules Robinson also created
the education department and established the Government Central
School, of which the late Colonial Secretary Dr. Frederick
Stewart, was the first head master.   The public works of the
Colony were also carried on energetically.   A water supply was
provided from the South side of the Island ; markets were built;
public gardens were laid out ; roads were extended, and a sum
of over two hundred thousand dollars was laid out in the
erection of a Mint which was abandoned under the succeeding
administration.

    There was a considerable decrease of crime during this
administration, although the years 1859, 1864, and 1865, were
an exception.   The reports of piracies and robberies were
exceptionally numerous in 1859 and again in 1864 and 1865.
On the night of the 28th January, 1864, the Danish brig, *Chico*,
while at anchor outside the harbour, was attacked by four
pirate junks.   The captain and two others were killed, the vessel
ransacked, and then set on fire and deserted.   Fortunately the
crew escaped.   In 1865, the Colony and adjacent waters were
infested by hordes of pirates, burglars, and hill robbers.   In
April, 1865, the Danish brig, *Georg Andrews*, bound to Swatow,
was boarded by pirates outside the Lymoon pass, the captain was
killed, others wounded, and part of the cargo, consisting of rice
(but which was supposed to have been opium), carried away.   The

pirates escaped. Burglaries by gangs, known as drain gangs, who quarried from the drains to the houses selected for attack, were also common in 1864 and 1865. In February, 1865, a drain gang burrowed under the Central Bank of Western India and, obtaining access to the Bank treasury, succeeded in abstracting over one hundred thousand dollars in notes and gold bullion. In the month of June following, a rather more serious skirmish than usual took place, at Aberdeen, between the police and some fifty burglars or pirates, and a few of both parties were killed and wounded, but only four or five of the rascals were apprehended. Some good work was done by the *Opossum* and *Haughty* gunboats in the destruction and capture of pirates. The state of the Colony at this time may be imagined from an official notification issued on the 1st April, 1865 :—" Every Chinese going out after dark must carry a light. From 8 p.m. till morning gunfire, any Chinese found without a pass and light will be taken into custody."

Sir Richard Graves MacDonnell arrived as Governor and took over the administration of the Colony from Mr. Mercer, on the 11th March, 1866. Sir Richard MacDonnell became known as the severe Governor and was much feared by the Chinese. His first measure, which was a popular one, was to revise the constitution of the Legislative Council by the appointment of an additional unofficial member, in pursuance of the powers he had brought out with him for the purpose. He became still more popular with the mercantile community by his energetic measures to repress piracy, which at the time of his arrival was the cause of frequent loss of life and of considerable interference with trade, especially the native junk trade. He established branches of the Harbour Office at the outlying villages round the coast lines of Hongkong and Kowloon, where pirate junks resorted, passed a new Chinese Registration Ordinance, and urged the Naval authorities and the Viceroy of Canton to more systematic and combined efforts for the suppression of piracy.

Sir Richard MacDonnell also took in hand the question of gambling, the number of Chinese gambling houses in the Colony being a principal source of corruption in the police force. After the failure of efforts to suppress the gambling houses, he announced that the Government of Hongkong had come to the resolution of tolerating gambling houses for the Chinese, under severe restrictions. This announcement met with general public approval, and licensed gambling houses, paying a heavy fee for the monopoly, were opened. The licence fees amounted, in less than three years, to three hundred thousand dollars, but by this time public opinion had entirely changed and the Governor was obliged to close the houses and separate the revenue from the general revenue of the Colony, as a special fund for the exclusive benefit of the Chinese. A large portion of this fund was afterwards granted to the Tung Wa Hospital which was opened in February, 1872, as a purely Chinese hospital. This hospital is still carried on under a directorate of Chinese gentlemen elected annually.

From the summer of 1866 to the end of 1868 was a period of great commercial depression which naturally affected seriously the revenue, more particularly as the Colony had been called upon to pay an annual military contribution of £20,000 to the Imperial Government of the Colony. At the beginning of the depression Sir Richard MacDonnell introduced a Stamp Ordinance as a means of assisting the revenue, and carried it against the expressed wishes of the community. He also stopped the expenditure on public works and discontinued the mint. As the commercial crises became more pronounced, the Governor was blamed as the cause of the supposed impending ruin of the Colony, the chief reasons for the blame being his support of the

Imperial demands for the annual military contribution, his stamp ordinance, and the failure of his attempts to remove the Chinese Customs' stations at the throat gates of the Colony, which operated as a blockade of the port. At the commencement of the year 1869 however, the increase in the number of shipping and the development of new enterprises showed that the commercial depression was over, and then Sir Richard MacDonnell was as much praised as he was before blamed.

The so-called blockade of the port by Chinese Customs' (likin) stations was the cause of energetic protests by Sir Richard MacDonnell, but no great success resulted, and when Sir Rutherford Alcock, the then British Minister to China, advised the establishment of a Chinese consulate in Hongkong as a means of removing the blockade, and justified his suggestion by stating that Hongkong was confessedly a great smuggling depôt, Sir Richard MacDonnell at once took the part of the mercantile community and strongly defended the reputation of the Colony. He also supported the interests of the legitimate trade in the emigration of Chinese from Hongkong, as distinguished from the Macao coolie traffic which was denounced as a form of slave trade.

During the absence of Sir Richard Graves MacDonnell, in 1869, the Government of the Colony was administered by Major General Whitfeild as Lieutenant-Governor.

On the 18th March, 1869, the Suez Canal was opened for traffic, but the wonderful change effected in commerce by the shortening of the route from Europe to Asia, by means of the Canal, was not realized in Hongkong until a few years later. The success of the Suez Canal was generally not believed in, and the prospect of its becoming even in a small way the channel of trade between the East and the West was not dreamed of. The most that was admitted was that it might compete with the Egyptian Railway by transporting some of the merchandize in.

barges. The fallacy of these views was, however, made apparent as steamers were attracted to the new route by the great saving of time and distance it afforded.

Sir Richard MacDonnell left the Colony, in 1872, to the regret of the community, and was succeeded in his administration by Sir Arthur Kennedy, who arrived on the 16th April, 1872, and soon endeared himself to all classes of the community by his urbanity and the kindness of his disposition, and became one of the most popular of Governors.

The effect upon the commerce of the Colony caused by the opening of the Suez Canal and the completion of telegraphic communication between Hongkong and Europe, which placed Hongkong in communication with the whole commercial world, was beginning to be realized at the commencement of Sir Arthur Kennedy's administration. A period of prosperity arrived, and the Colony began to go ahead, but the prosperity was not all real and a serious commercial depression followed from 1874 to 1876.

The inadequacy of the water supply to the increasing inhabitants was occasionally severely felt during Sir Arthur Kennedy's period of office, and a new water-works scheme was mooted. This scheme ultimately developed into the present magnificent supply of water from Tytam, but the works were not commenced until 1883.

An extensive system of tree planting all over the island was commenced by Sir Arthur Kennedy with the view of improving the healthiness of the Colony and to render the appearance of the hills less barren, but nothing further was done to alleviate the insanitary condition under which the Colony was suffering.

During the night of the 22nd and 23rd September, 1874, the most furious typhoon ever known in the annals of the Colony occurred. The storm was appalling and the destruction to shipping in the harbour and to buildings on shore and loss of life was unprecedented and could not have been anticipated. The same storm swept over Macao and did great havoc there, from which it is hardly yet recovered, but the advancing spirit of Hongkong soon removed all traces of its fury there.

The year 1874 was also noted for the piratical attack on the *Spark*, one of the river steamers of the Hongkong, Canton, and Macao Steamboat Company. The *Spark* was on her way from Canton to Macao when a number of pirates, who had gone on board as passengers, rose, at a given signal, and murdered the Captain and all the foreigners on board, except one who was so badly injured that his recovery was surprising. A pirate junk then ranged alongside and took off the murderers and the valuable portion of the cargo. It is satisfactory to record that after a long search all the pirates were ultimately captured and executed in Canton.

Sir Arthur Kennedy left the Colony in 1877, much beloved by the inhabitants, by whom he was called the good Sir Arthur. His memory is perpetuated by a statue erected in the Botanic Gardens.

Sir John Pope Hennessy arrived, as Sir Arthur Kennedy's successor, on the 22nd April, 1877, and held the reins of Government until March, 1882. His policy, as expressed by him on his arrival, was to follow in the footsteps of Sir Arthur Kennedy and to protect the mercantile interests of the Colony. Sir John Pope Hennessy, however, soon began to espouse the cause of the natives (Chinese) as against the English (foreigners) and created such friction with the European portion of the population that he ultimately became socially isolated from it. The meetings of the Legislative Council were scenes of strife between the Governor and the unofficial members, and contrasted strangely with the

E

previously calm period of Sir Arthur Kennedy's administration. The views of Sir John Pope Hennessy were directly opposed to the views and wishes of the British community in regard to public works, the system of education, the treatment of criminals, and the restriction of the Chinese from what was known as the European quarter of the city. He looked upon the English merchants as so many interlopers with no permanent home or family ties in the Colony. They were, he considered, to Hongkong what the Chinese are to Australia. They did not go to the Colony to settle, but to make money as quickly as possible and to get away in a few years, and that the real interests of the Colony were being sacrificed to these rolling stone speculators ; and it was these people, who, though a very small minority, and with very little capital of their own, had influence enough to get an Order in Council passed prohibiting the Queen's Chinese subjects of Hongkong from using the best commercial quarters of the town. The administration of Sir John Pope Hennessy was apparently a financial success. By curtailing expenditure and stopping all public works which could possibly be postponed and by keeping up a high rate of taxation, a considerable surplus of revenue over expenditure was accumulated.

The year 1878 was noted for the number of burglaries committed in Hongkong—the most remarkable of them was a night attack, on the 25th September, 1878, by a large gang of armed men upon a Chinese bank in Wing Lok Street. They successfully held the street while the building was plundered and escaped with their booty without any of the number being caught.

The increase in crime was popularly considered to be the effect of the Governor's alteration in the method of treating Chinese criminals. The much greater leniency of the prison regulations introduced by Sir John Pope Hennessy, gave him, among the Chinese criminals, the name of the " merciful man."

One of the greatest conflagrations known in the Colony happened on Christmas Day, 1878, the remembrance of which is still fresh. As many as 365 houses were destroyed by this great fire, and some lives were lost.

The sanitary condition of the Colony was the subject of much discussion with Governor Hennessy and many hard words were used. The military authorities took up the question and represented the great importance of it to the War Office. The Secretary of State for the Colonies thereupon sent out Mr. O. Chadwick to report and advise, with the result that the grand system of water supply from Taitam and a new system of drainage were commenced in the next administration.

Sir John Pope Hennessy left the Colony on the 7th March, 1882, and the Government was then administered by Mr. (now Sir) William Marsh, the then Colonial Secretary, until the arrival of Sir George Ferguson Bowen, as Governor, on the 30th March, 1883.

The administration of Sir William Marsh put an end to the turmoils occasioned by Sir John Pope Hennessy's policy. Public works, long deferred, were started and carried on with vigour. Among the most important works commenced in this period with which the name of Mr. J. M. Price, the then Surveyor-General, will be ever associated, were the Taitam reservoir, tunnel, and conduit (the surface of the latter now forming the Bowen Road—a favourite walk for the people); the Victoria College; a breakwater at Causeway Bay—forming a refuge for boats in stormy weather ; and at Kowloon the Observatory and Water Police Station.

The administration of Sir George Ferguson Bowen lasted from March, 1883, to December, 1885. His first work was the reorganisation of the Legislative Council on a partly representative basis, one of the unofficial members being elected by the Chamber of Commerce and one by the unofficial Justices of the Peace. The effect of the new constitution was considered to place Hongkong on the direct road to a self-elected responsible government. The balance of legislative power is, however, in the hands of the Governor through a majority of official members, and the only real effect of the reconstitution hitherto has been to increase the number of members of the Legislative Council without altering the strength of the official majority. Prior to Sir George Bowen's scheme of reconstruction, the Legislative Council consisted of four official and four unofficial members, and afterwards of six official and five unofficial members—three of the latter (one being a Chinese) being appointed by the Queen, on the recommendation of the Governor, and the remaining two being elected as above mentioned. The health of the colony received great attention during Sir George Bowen's administration and a Public Health Ordinance was passed dealing with the erection and drainage of buildings, food supply, and nuisances, and, what is of great importance, the establishment of a Sanitary Board for the carrying out of the provisions of the Health Ordinance. The Tytam waterworks were also carried on with vigour, an abundant supply of water being absolutely necessary for the proper working of the new laws.

The strained relations between France and China culminated, in 1884, in France taken hostile measures against China. France declared she was not at war with China but simply protecting her colonies against China by means of reprisals. The bombardment of Keelung, Formosa, by the French on the 5th August, 1884, and the hostile preparations of the Chinese, shewed that France and China had drifted into actual warfare. Great Britain proclaimed her neutrality, and Hongkong, in consequence, became closed to a large trade which had risen in the supply of the combatants with their provisions and all kinds of stores—warlike and otherwise.

The city of Victoria inclosed at this time as many as ten thousand armed men from the mainland, waiting for an opportunity to plunder, and on the morning of the 3rd October, 1884, under the pretence that some coolies had been fined for breach of the nutrality regulations,—a rising of the roughs occurred. The whole of the police force was engaged in attempting to quell the disturbance and, having no reserve, some companies of the East Kent Regiment (the Buffs) then stationed at Hongkong, marched, fully armed and with fixed bayonets, to the spreading disturbance, when the rioters quickly hid themselves and dispersed, before they had effected any real damage. Several ringleaders were captured and deported and measures adopted to disarm all persons found carrying arms, and to prevent the carrying of arms, without special licence, in the future. The only other effect upon the Colony of the Franco-Chinese war was a strike of all the cargo-boat people (under the pretext that some of them would be required in the loading or unloading of the French Mail Steamers),—and a temporary stoppage of the supply of provisions —chiefly vegetables—from Canton ; these difficulties were soon arranged, but it was a great relief to the Colony when, on the 6th April, 1885, peace was declared between France and China and all further trouble was thereby removed.

Another attack by pirates—similar to the attack on the steamer *Spark* in 1874—was made, in 1884, on the steamer *Greyhound* a few hours after leaving Hongkong. A number of pirates went on board as passengers from Hongkong and—when the steamer was approaching some junks which were stationed at the place on the steamer's course where the attack was to be made—the Captain was shot and thrown overboard by the pirates, who then took possession of the steamer and loaded the junks with their plunder. The pirates then made off in the junks, while the steamer was worked back to Hongkong by some of the crew who were thought by the pirates to have been disabled during the attack.

Sir George Bowen left the Colony on the 19th December, 1885, when the Government was again administered by Sir William Marsh.

During the winter of 1885–86, great complaints were made as to the overcrowding of the city of Victoria, and the remarkable hording together of the Chinese, and that if the sanitary measures proposed by the then newly constituted Sanitary Board were adopted, large numbers of people would be rendered homeless and that even then some were obliged to sleep in the streets. Sir William Marsh thereupon appointed a Land Commission, with Sir George Phillippo, the then Chief Justice, as Chairman, to inquire into and report upon any means that could be adopted by the Government in the disposal of land to check overcrowding in the more thickly populated parts of the city. The Commission made its report the following year, and among other recommendations for enlarging the area in which people can live in Hongkong, recommended a moderate system of reclamation by the Government from the harbour, in suitable places. This recommendation gave rise, two years afterwards, to the gigantic scheme of Mr. Catchick Paul Chater and other large marine lot holders for a grand praya reclamation along the whole front of the city from the military barracks to West Point, a distance of nearly two miles.

Sir William Marsh left the Colony in April, 1886, and was succeeded in the administration of the Government by Lieutenant-General W. Gordon Cameron, C.B. the senior military officer in command, until the arrival of Governor Sir G. William Des Vœux on the 6th October, 1887.

In 1886 the question of the " Hongkong blockade " was considered by a Commission appointed by the English and Chinese governments to inquire into the question of the prevention of smuggling into China from Hongkong. The Commission sat in Hongkong and was composed of Mr. (now Sir James) Russell, then Puisne Judge of Hongkong; Sir Robert Hart, Inspector General of Chinese Customs, and Shao Taotai, joint Commissioners for China; and Mr. Byron Brenan, Her Majesty's Consul at Tientsin, who represented the Indian Government. After discussion, Sir James Russell formulated the basis of an Agreement between the Commissioners, providing for the registration of the movement of opium to and from Hongkong, on equivalent measures being arranged between China and Macao, and also providing for the settlement of any complaints made by junks trading with Hongkong against the native Customs' revenue stations or cruisers in the neighbourhood of the Colony. The Agreement was signed by the Commissioners on the 11th September, 1886, and an ordinance providing for the registration and movement of opium was passed the following year, since which time little has been heard of the Hongkong blockade, although the native Chinese Customs' stations still surround the Colony.

At the time of the arrival of Sir William Des Vœux the Colony was progressing with rapid—too rapid—strides in population, shipping, commercial activity, and apparent prosperity. Numerous limited companies were formed under the Companies' Ordinances, for all manner of undertakings, mining, planting, and industrial; and to such an extent were all classes of the community carried away by this wave of activity and prosperity, that the Colony felt itself powerful and competent enough to extend its control and investments in planting and mining companies to Borneo, the Straits Settlements, Tonquin, Australia and America. Sir William Des Vœux was so impressed with the great progress of the Colony that he penned glowing accounts to the Secretary of State of the position, beauty, and wealth of Hongkong.

The first damper soon came in the shape of directions from the Secretary of State to the Governor to increase the military contribution by £20,000 making in all £40,000 per annum. The Colony protested through the unofficial members of Council, but without avail, and then the Governor was blamed as the cause of the additional exaction, through his over-glowing statements as to the prosperity of the Colony.

The Praya Reclamation Ordinance was passed in 1889, and this great work was commenced soon afterwards.

One of the greatest achievements of Sir William Des Vœux was his enactment for the prevention of fires. The number of fires, accidental or the work of incendiaries, had increased to such an alarming extent, that the fire brigades were almost constantly at work and some serious accidents had happened. The Ordinance passed by Sir William Des Vœux simply provided that an inquiry should be held into the cause of each fire and that, from the time of the happening of the fire to the conclusion of the inquiry, the buildings and property where the fire happened should be kept in the custody of the police. The effect of this was magical, fires suddenly ceased and from that time the number of fires has been exceedingly small in proportion to the number of occupied buildings, to the great delight and gain of the Fire Insurance Companies.

The Colony celebrated the Queen's Jubilee in right royal manner on the 9th November, 1887. The Chinese entered into the spirit of the celebration with great good-will, collecting, among themselves, and spending over one hundred thousand dollars on the celebration, a very gratifying assurance of their appreciation of the just and liberal government of the British Crown.

The question of an additional lighthouse to render the approach to the Colony from the South safe at all times, and

enable ships to came right up to the harbour by night, was settled
with the Chinese Government in the year 1888, by their granting
permission for the erection of a lighthouse on Gap rock, about
forty miles to the South of the Island. The works were
completed and the light started in 1892. It is a white flash-
light, and can be well seen at night from all the hills commanding
a view over the South side of Hongkong. Arrangements are now
(1893) being made for the erection of another lighthouse on
Waglan Island, off the East coast of Hongkong, as a guide to
steamers coming from the North and East.

The year 1889 was notable for the heaviest thunder-storm
that has ever been known to visit Hongkong, or any other
place. The worst part of the storm was during the night of the
29th of May. Forty inches of rain fell during this storm; the
streets were torn up, trees uprooted, and some houses were carried
away by the flood of waters; the Queen's Road was raised several
feet by the sand brought down from the hills, and damage done to
the extent of two hundred thousand dollars. Several lives were
lost in this storm both by the lightning and by the force of the
torrents formed during the storm.

Sir William Des Vœux left for England on the 19th February,
1890, and Mr. (now Sir) Francis Fleming, Colonial Secretary,
was on the same day sworn in as the Officer Administering
the Government, during his absence.

The Duke and Duchess of Connaught arrived, on the
31st March, 1890, from India on their way to England, *viâ*
America, and were received with every manifestation of festive
good-will by all sections of the community, including the Chinese
who invited them to an elegant dinner in native style—which
was accepted to the great pleasure of the Chinese.—The Duke
of Connaught laid the memorial stone of the great Praya
Reclamation Works on the 2nd April, 1890, Mr. Chater, the

originator of the scheme, delivering an address on the occasion in which he stated it was the desire of the people that the new road to be formed along the line of the present Praya should be named after him as Connaught Road.

The year 1891 was noted for another tragedy at the hands of a band of pirates who went on board the Douglas steamer *Namoa* as passengers. When the *Namoa* had proceeded about fifty miles on her voyage to the Coast Ports, and the Captain and passengers were at tiffin, the pirates disclosed their true colors and took possession of the bridge and engine-room. They then shot the Captain (who died a few hours afterwards), and made the passengers prisoners, while the steamer and passengers were looted and the loot placed in junks which were ready in waiting. The pirates then left in the junks, after rendering the boats useless and attempting to disable the engines, in which, fortunately, they did not succeed. The steamer returned to Hongkong, but the pirates escaped in the darkness of the night. Some of the pirates, who were believed to form a portion of the gang which attacked the *Greyhound* in a similar manner seven years previously, were afterwards captured by the Chinese authorities and beheaded at Kowloon City.

Sir William Des Vœux returned to the Colony in February 1891, to find that the commercial activity which prevailed during the early part of his administration had come to a standstill. Many of the Companies—particularly Planting and Mining Companies whose field of work was outside the Colony—were in a bad way, and it was beginning to be felt that the millions of dollars sent out of the Colony for these speculations would never return. The fluctuations in exchange and a continual fall in the price of silver affected commercial transactions to a very large extent and the Colony began to enter into one of the periodical commercial depressions with which it is now familiar, but from which it never learns any lessons. Systematic gambling in shares was suddenly brought to an end by the passing of an Ordinance— brought before the Legislative Council by Mr. James J. Keswick of the house of Messrs. Jardine, Matheson & Co.—to render illegal contracts for sale and purchase of shares where the numbers of the shares were not stated in the contracts.

The Governor was again blamed as the cause of saddling the community with the increased military contribution – through his glowing descriptions of the position and wealth of the Colony— and this led to the Governor, in an address to the Legislative Council, delivering what was called a counter blast to the blast of the unofficial members, in which he further asserted the truth of his former descriptions of the sound and progressive state of the Colony.

Sir William Des Vœux left Hongkong for good, on account of his health, on the 7th May, 1891, and during his absence and until the arrival of Sir William Robinson as Governor in December, 1891, the administration of the Government devolved on Major-General Digby Barker, the senior military officer in command.

Sir William Robinson arrived at the time when the most serious depression that has ever visited the Colony was at its greatest. The values of local stocks and shares had shrunk by a few million dollars; the fluctuations in exchange had curtailed business, chiefly that of importers, to a very large extent; over- building in the preceding period of prosperity had produced a great number of empty houses and lowered the rents of all occupied dwellings—the rents of which had been raised in the days of overcrowding; enterprise was at a standstill for want of the funds sent out of the Colony—in its days of prosperity—in profitless mining and planting ventures, and the outlook into the future was very gloomy. Sir William Robinson has expressed his belief in the soundness of the position of the Colony and that, notwithstanding the diminution of the ordinary revenue of the Colony over its expenditure by the recent great increase in the military contribution, he will be able to leave the Colony with a considerable surplus of revenue.

Reviewing the whole history of Hongkong it will be found that the Colony has more than fulfilled the purpose for which it was ceded in 1841. From a barren rock it has rapidly risen to be a possession of immense importance to the trade of Great Britain with China; lying directly in contact with the Chinese Empire, in communication with all countries of the world, and governed by the broad principles of English liberty, justice, and humanity, the improving influence of Hongkong is surely, though silently, extending into the vast Empire which it touches, and in proportion to its growth, its commanding influence will extend.

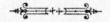

CHAPTER VII.

PEDDER'S WHARF is the principal landing pier in the Colony and is situated at the foot of Pedder's Street, the most central portion of the City of Victoria. It is built of wood and has a length of two hundred and fifty feet jutting into the harbour, and on either side of the pier are two landing stairs. Here the visitor will be brought, after his steamer is safely moored in the harbour, by a launch from one of the Hotels, or if the steamer goes to the wharves at Kowloon, belonging to the Hongkong Wharf and Godown Company, the visitor may cross the harbour to Pedder's Wharf by one of the ferry launches which run every quarter of an hour between the two places. Pedder's wharf is an exceedingly busy place. Steam-launches, sampans (the native Chinese boats), and boats of all descriptions are constantly arriving and departing with passengers and others, of all nationalities, bound to the shipping lying in the harbour, to Kowloon on the opposite shore, or other places on the island, making Pedder's Wharf an animated scene at all times of the day.

HOTELS.

The leading Hotels are the *Hongkong* and *Victoria*, in the City, and the *Mount Austin* at the Peak.

The Hongkong Hotel is immediately across the road (called the Praya) at Pedder's Wharf, and is centrally situated opposite the General Post Office. The principal entrance is on the left-hand side of Pedder's Street, leading up from Pedder's Wharf to Queen's Road Central. The building is six stories high and of magnificent proportions. The numerous bedrooms are lofty and well ventilated and open on to spacious verandahs. The accommodation is extensive and complete and comprises reading, writing, smoking, and billiard rooms, and ladies' dining and drawing rooms. The Hotel steam-launch conveys passengers and baggage to and from all mail steamers. The Hotel is the property of and is carried on by the Hongkong Hotel Co., Ld.

The Victoria Hotel is also a first-class hotel situated in the central part of the City, adjoining Pottinger Street, the next Street westward of Pedder's Street, with entrances from Queen's Road Central, Praya Central, and Pottinger Street. It has 40 commodious and well-furnished bedrooms, a spacious dining room overlooking the harbour, sitting, reading, billiard, and smoking rooms. The proprietors are Messrs. Dorabjee and Hing Kee, formerly the lessees of the Hongkong Hotel.

The Mount Austin Hotel is magnificiently situated at the Peak, above Victoria Gap, and, although 1,400 feet above sea level, can be reached in a quarter of an hour from the City by means of the High Level Tramway. The salubrity of the situation, which commands a most beautiful outlook over the numerous islands to the South and West of Hongkong, are recommendations of great value to this Hotel. The building is a pleasing and conspicuous object, on the crest of the mountain, when viewed from the deck of steamers arriving from the South. The Hotel has extensive and complete accommodation for visitors and families, and the building contains lofty and well-designed drawing and dining rooms as well as reading, smoking, and billiard rooms. The Hotel belongs to and is managed by the Austin Arms Hotel and Building Co., Ld.

There are also the *Windsor Hotel*, a private hotel or boarding house in Connaught House, Queen's Road Central, the *Peak Hotel*, at the upper terminus of the Tramway, 1,200 feet above the sea level, and hotels or inns of less pretensions in the heart of the city.

There is also a very comfortable and well managed private boarding house very pleasantly situated at Nos. 1 to 3, Victoria View, Kowloon.

PLACES OF WORSHIP.

St. John's Cathedral.—St. John's Church (Anglican) is situated just above the parade ground, Queen's Road Central. It is a cruciform edifice built in the gothic style, with a handsome square tower erected over the western porch. The eastern window is a large handsome window of stained glass and a pleasing feature of the building. There is also a memorial window erected to the late Dr. Stewart, formerly Colonial Secretary, in the northern side of the building. St. John's Cathedral is capable of seating some 800 people and possesses a very fine organ.

The foundation stone of the building was laid in March 1847.

The Roman Catholic Cathedral (church of the Immaculate Conception).—This is a handsome modern cruciform structure in the gothic style and, from its position above the Caine Road and centre of the city, is conspicuous from the harbour. The short square tower with small steeple is erected over the transept. The building is vested in the Vicar Apostolic of the Roman Catholic Church in Hongkong. The Right Reverend John T. Raimondi, D.D., Bishop of Acantho, is the present Vicar Apostolic.

The Union (Protestant) Church.—This Church, sometimes called the Scotch Church, is erected along the Kennedy Road, adjoining the tramway and not far from the public gardens. It is a pleasant looking building of the Italian style and is capable of accommodating some 500 people. It is vested in trustees for the seatholders and the management is in the hands of a committee. The minister's house adjoins the church. The present minister is the Reverend G. H. Bondfield of the London Missionary Society.

St. Joseph's (Roman Catholic) Church.—This is a small church in the Garden Road above the lower terminus of the tramway, and was originally built for the English-speaking portion of the Roman Catholic Community. The present building was erected in 1876 on the site of the former church which was destroyed by the great typhoon of 1874. There are school buildings attached to this church.

St. Peter's Church.—This is a Mission Church for seamen, Praya West, and adjoins the Sailor's Home. The building is of moderate size and carries a spire, which forms a pleasing addition to the view from the western portion of the harbour.

German Bethesda Chapel.—This simple but pleasant building is attached to the Berlin Ladies' Foundling Hospital, just below the Bonham Road, which runs above the western portion of the town. A special and interesting Christmas service is held here every Christmas Eve for the benefit of the children.

SCHOOLS.

The subject of education, particularly the education of the Chinese, has received great attention from the Government and large sums of money are annually spent in Government grants.

Victoria College.—This is a Government school for instruction in English and Chinese. The number of scholars is about 1,000, the large majority of whom are Chinese. The fees range from $1 to $3 per month for each boy, but the greater proportion of the cost of keeping up the college and staff is borne by the Government. The handsome college buildings are situated above the Hollywood Road, in the central and Chinese portion of the city. The college, which has superseded the old "Central School," was opened on the 10th July, 1889.

St. Joseph's (Roman Catholic) College.—This is a large and handsome building above the Roman Catholic Cathedral, the principal entrance is from Robinson Road. A large number of Portuguese children are educated at this establishment, which is under the management of the Christian Brothers.

The Diocesan Home and Orphanage is situated just below the Bonham Road in the western portion of the city. This school is principally for the care and education of Eurasians. It belongs to the Church of England and is managed by a committee, of which the Right Rev. Bishop Burdon, Bishop of Victoria, is Chairman.

St. Paul's College is a neat and attractive-looking building at College Gardens where Glenealy commences. It comprises a school for Chinese, under the management of Bishop Burdon.

There are many other schools in the Colony belonging to the Government and to the various mission and educational bodies, including the French Convent, situated in Queen's Road East, and the Italian Convent in Caine Road.

PUBLIC BUILDINGS.

Government House, now the official residence of Governor Sir William Robinson, K.C.M.G., is pleasantly situated on high ground above St. John's Cathedral. It is a square granite building, with ball-room attached, and commands views over the harbour and to the mountains of the mainland from its northern side and of Victoria Peak and the range of hills adjacent from its southern side. Government House stands in its own grounds, which are laid out in garden walks and tennis courts.

F

Head-Quarter House is erected on the hill to the east of St. John's Cathedral, and immediately above the military barracks. It is the residence of the Commander-in-Chief of the military forces of the Far East and is now occupied by Major-General G. Digby Barker, C.B.

The Government Offices are close to St. John's Cathedral on its western side. It is a building of two stories and comprises, on the upper floor, the Executive and Legislative Council Chambers and the offices of the Governor and Colonial Secretary. On the ground floor are the offices of the Director of Public Works and Public Works Department.

The City Hall is one of the principal buildings and is an ornament to the city. It comprises the Theatre Royal, a commodious and elegant theatre, a valuable library and reading rooms, a museum containing a large collection of Asiatic fauna— the birds, snakes, and insects, being exceedingly valuable and interesting. The City Hall also contains large and elegant rooms for balls and public assemblies.

The Hongkong and Shanghai Bank.—This great local institution is housed in a magnificent domed building next to the City Hall, and is one of the finest structures in the colony.

The General Post Office is situated at the junction of Queen's Road Central and Pedder Street. It is a large square granite building with verandahs supported by stone pillars. Letters are delivered from the side facing Pedder Street and are posted at the side facing Queen's Road Central. The entrance to the Post Office and Money Order Office is from Pedder Street at the rear of the building. The offices of the Colonial Treasury are over the Post Office.

The Clock Tower, at the top of Pedder Street and over against the Post Office, obstructing the traffic, is one of the few monuments erected in Hongkong by public subscription. It was erected in 1862, the fine illuminated clock being the gift of the firm of Messrs. Douglas Lapraik & Co.

The Supreme Court is a plain building of granite supported by stone columns. The Courts are upstairs and are interesting to visit during the criminal sessions – which commence on the 18th of each month--or during the trial of a native case.

The Hongkong Club stands opposite to the Supreme Court buildings and Post Office, on the other side of Queen's Road Central. It is a commodious structure of three stories with wide verandahs. The Club possesses an excellent library and, from its central position, is largely used as an exchange by its members.

The Club Germania is situated in Wyndham Street, which runs up from the East side of the Hongkong Club to the commencement of Glenealy. It is a substantial building with a concert hall in addition to the usual club rooms. It was erected, as its name implies, by the German members of the community.

The Lusitano Club is in Shelly Street on the higher level of Caine Road. It belongs to the Portuguese community and the building contains a good concert room, as well as library and reading rooms.

The Government Civil Hospital is a splendid series of buildings situated in the western division of the city on high ground above Queen's Road West. This hospital is under the charge of the Government Medical Department and is a striking testimony of the care of the Government for its sick and wounded officers. In addition to the wards in which various diseases are located, and wards for police and Board of Trade cases, there are several rooms for private individuals who can have every medical comfort and convenience at a reasonable cost. The Civil Hospital is one of the most worthy institutions under the control of the Government.

The Alice Memorial Hospital was founded a few years ago by Dr. Ho Kai to the memory of the late Mrs. Ho Kai. It is situated in Staunton Street not far from Victoria College. The hospital, which is chiefly for Chinese, is under the management of the London Missionary Society and is supported by endowments granted by that Society, Dr. Ho Kai, Mr. Belilios, and other public benefactors, and by voluntary public subscriptions.

The Tung Wa (Chinese) Hospital and Lunatic Asylum is situated in Po Yan Street in the heart of the district of Tai-pingshan, the principal Chinese quarter of the city. It was opened in February, 1872, for Chinese patients only, who prefer to be under Chinese medical treatment. The Tung Wa Hospital is an incorporated body and is under the management of a directorate of Chinese gentlemen, who are elected annually.

Victoria Gaol is a large granite building of various wings springing from a common centre, occupying valuable ground on a higher level in the centre of the city. It is approached direct from Pottinger Street leading up the hill from the Victoria Hotel. The average number of prisoners is about 550.

The Magistracy is located in a building immediately adjoining Victoria Gaol.

The Observatory is situated on Mount Elgin, Kowloon peninsula, and was established for physical research and record. The building was completed in the year 1883 and records were commenced on the 1st January, 1884. In addition to monthly and yearly weather reports, a China Coast Meteorological Register is published twice a day, at 10 a.m. and 4 p.m., with weather forecasts. The electric time-ball, at Kowloon Point, is dropped daily at 1 p.m. (Sundays and holidays excepted) by the Mean Time Clock at the Observatory. Magnetic observations are also recorded at the Observatory, and in times of stormy weather, meteorological signals are hoisted on the mast beside the time-ball, and these signals are repeated from the Commodore's receiving ship, the *Victor Emanuel*, and from the mast over the main entrance of the buildings, at Kowloon, of the Hongkong and Kowloon Wharf and Godown Company, Limited.

Docks.

The Docks are the property of the Hongkong and Whampoa Dock Company, Limited, and are the most extensive of any in Asia. The principal docks, known as the Kowloon Docks, are situated at Hunghom, a village on the Kowloon peninsula across the bay east of Kowloon point. Vessels of 550 feet in length and 30 feet draft of water can be docked at Kowloon. Here also are the engineers' steam workshops, saw-mill, and foundry, and a patent slip which can haul up vessels in 2½ hours. These docks are well worthy of a visit, which can be made at any time by arrangement with the courteous Secretary and Manager or Assistant Manager. The Company has also a large dock (the Cosmopolitan Dock) and workshops at the village of Samshuipo on the north-west side of the Kowloon peninsula ; and two docks (Hope and Lament docks) and workshops at Aberdeen on the south side of Hongkong island.

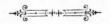

CHAPTER VIII.

The Tramway.—Victoria Peak.—Water supply.—Visit to the Happy Valley
and Cemeteries.—The China Pony.—Continuation of the Journey to
Taitam reservoir.—Stanley and Wong-ma Kok.

THE visitor will probably select Victoria Peak as the
first place of interest to visit after his arrival in
Hongkong, particularly if the day is fine and the hills
are clear of mist. The High Level Tramway will take the visitor
from St. John's—the lower terminus in Garden Road, a hundred
yards or so above St. John's Cathedral—to Victoria Gap—the
upper terminus, at a height of 1,300 feet above sea level—in nine
minutes, and this is the most comfortable means of making the
journey. The trams run every quarter of an hour, except during
the middle of the day, and the first class return fare is only
50 cents.

The tramway is the outcome of the rapid growth of villa
residences in the Peak district, erected by merchants and others
to escape from the heat of the city during the summer months
and enjoy a night's sleep in the pure and cooler air of the
mountains.

The Peak tramway is interesting as being the first cable
railway in Asia. This important work was first begun on the
20th September, 1885, and was opened for public traffic on the
30th May, 1888. On leaving the lower terminus the incline is
so gradual that it is hardly noticeable, and one experiences the
pleasure of moving along in the car on a smooth track without
any visible motive power. The flexible plough steel cable in
front shews that the motive power is somewhere in the heights
above. The sylvan scenery, at the commencement of the ascent,

is refreshing and beautiful. At Kennedy Road there is a station, and soon after passing it the incline begins to get steeper, and at Bowen Road station the steepest incline of 1 in 2 appears in view. Any apprehensions as to being able to keep one's seat comfortable in ascending this steep hill are soon dispelled. The seats are firmly fixed to the floor of the car and always maintain the same position in relation to the car itself. The sensation is therefore the same in travelling up steep ascents or on the level, except that the houses, trees, and the hills themselves appear to incline backwards in a most startling manner. Near to the top of the steepest incline the halfway cross-siding is reached and the descending car is passed, then another short steep part and the line takes a curve towards the Gap. There is another station at Plantation Road and from this altitude the view down to the harbour and across the harbour to the mountains of the mainland is magnificent. A minute or two more and the car glides on the level into the upper terminus. Here the visitor may, by the courtesy of the engineer in charge, inspect the engines, boilers, and machinery employed in bringing the car to the top of the line. The steel cable, to the two ends of which the cars are attached, is seen to run round the winding drums, which are 8 feet in diameter. A pair of pointers travelling along a rectangular dial, in the engine room, and geared off the winding drum shaft shews to the engineer the exact position of the cars in motion on the line. The length of the line is 4,690 feet, and the height of the upper above the lower terminus in 1,207 feet. The easiest gradient is 1 in 25 and the steepest 1 in 2.

THE PEAK.

The Peak Hotel is just above the upper terminus. Chairs, which are waiting outside, will convey the visitor to any place he may choose to go. The path to the summit of Victoria Peak and the Signal Station, which is 500 feet higher than Victoria Gap, is the ascending path right in front of the Tramway Station leading under the Mount Austin Hotel erected on the hill above. There are several roads or bridle paths taking their directions from Victoria Gap. The path leading down on the North or City side of the Gap is the Peak Road, leading down direct to Queen's Gardens, Robinson Road, and the Botanic Gardens. The path leading down to the Pokfulam reservoir, which is seen at the foot of the valley on the south side of the Gap, joins the main road leading from Victoria to Aberdeen and the villages on the south side of the island, and the road along the southern spur of the hills to the left leads to Mount Kellet and down to Aberdeen. It also joins the Plantation Road and Magazine Gap Road and is frequently taken as a pleasant walk from the Peak to the City viâ Magazine Gap.

A good bridle path leads up from Victoria Gap to Victoria Peak where the Maritime Signal Station is situated. Passing the Mount Austin Hotel, a favorite resting place is soon reached called the Umbrella Seat. This seat is placed on a narrow saddle formed by the eastern ridge of Victoria Peak, and commands extensive and magnificent views over the harbour and mainland on the one side, and the China Sea and its numerous islands on the other side. After a ten minutes further climb Victoria Peak itself is reached, the commanding views from which, on a clear day, have been referred to in the first chapter. The visitor will not only be charmed with the extensive scenery, but will be interested in the signalling of the steamers and sailing vessels as they are sighted making for the harbour from all directions. If the steamer sighted should prove to be an English, French, American, or German Mail steamer, the intelligence will be announced by the firing of a cannon, in addition to the usual flag signals. The small building on the highest summit of the Peak was erected for meteorological instruments.

WATER SUPPLY.

A visit to the sources of the water supply of the city of Victoria is one of the most inviting excursions the island affords, and is attractive not only from the great interest the works themselves call forth, but from the charming variety of the island scenery brought to view in the ramble. The supply of water in the early days of the Colony was obtained from the small streamlets running down the different ravines, and as these mostly failed in the dry climate of the winter, when the north-east monsoon prevails, many wells were dug to increase the supply. The impurities contained in the water thus obtained in a tropical region in the most primitive manner will no doubt account in a large measure for the unhealthiness of the Colony in its younger days. It was not until the year 1860 that a serious effort was made to supply the inhabitants of Victoria with a constant supply of good water by properly constructed water-works, when the then Governor, Sir Hercules Robinson, offered a prize of $1,000 for the best plans of water-works for the Colony, and the prize was awarded to Mr. Rawlings of the department of Royal Engineers. The Pokfulam reservoir was then constructed and from that time, to the year 1888, the city of Victoria was dependent for its water supply on the yield of the Pokfulam catchment basin which is only 416 acres in extent. The reservoir at Pokfulam is capable of holding 68,000,000 gallons and the water is conveyed to the city by means of a masonry conduit two miles in length contouring the hill side at a level of about 460 feet above the sea.

These works furnished, in 1887, an average daily supply of $5\frac{3}{4}$ gallons per head for the entire population of the city, but the distribution works had—with the rapid growth of the city, especially in the upper levels—fallen far short of those required to effect an equal and economical distribution of the small quantity of water available.

In 1888 the construction of the new reservoir—situated in the Taitam valley, about 5 miles distant from the city—the piercing of the intervening range of hills by a tunnel 2,428 lineal yards in length, the construction of the conduit, filter beds, and service reservoir, brought within the limits of the city a further daily supply of about 2,500,000 gallons.

The catchment area of the Taitam reservoir is 700 acres and its contents 310,000,000 gallons. In 1890 a service reservoir, containing about 1,000,000 gallons and filter beds for filtering the supply derived from Pokfulam, were constructed at West Point.

The completion of these works rendered available, during any ordinary dry season, a minimum supply of 3,000,000 gallons per diem of filtered water.

During the last two years extensive works have been carried out for the better distribution of water within the city, in connection with which a greatly improved system of fire hydrants has been effected. Upwards of 20 miles of new water-mains, varying in size from 3 inches to 14 inches in diameter, with the necessary accessories, have been laid.

These service reservoirs have been constructed at levels of 700, 600, and 500 feet above sea level, into which filtered water is pumped by the hydraulic machinery installed in the pumping stations on the Bonham, Arbuthnot, and Garden Roads. These reservoirs are in connection with the mains supplying the higher levels of the city.

A constant supply of water is laid on into most of the houses, both in the European and Chinese districts, and street fountains have been erected, rendering a supply of water easily obtainable by those who do not avail themselves of a direct connection between their premises and the water-mains.

Prior to 1891 the Hill district, which includes Victoria Peak and Magazine Gap Point, and which has been annually becoming more popular for residential purposes, was entirely dependent for its water supply on wells.

During 1891 a complete system of water-mains was laid throughout this district, and pumping machinery was installed in the Bonham Road Pumping Station capable of lifting 40,000 gallons of water per diem to the highest part of the Peak, viz., 1,825 feet above sea level.

Filtered water is now constantly supplied throughout the Hill district at the same rates as are charged for water in the city of Victoria.

The way to the Taitam reservoir, starting from the Post Office—from which all the distances in the island are measured—can be taken either viâ the Queen's Road East, the Happy Valley, and Wongneichung Village, and the Stanley Road, or by way of the Bowen Road which leads into the Stanley Road by the western end of the tunnel. The visit will occupy a whole afternoon and will well repay the trouble, but for those who wish to avoid some steep hill climbing, a four coolie sedan-chair is desirable.

Starting by way of Queen's Road East the first buildings after passing the parade and cricket grounds are the military barracks, on both sides of the road ; then the Naval Yard follows on the left, and afterwards more barracks on both sides the road. Wellington Battery, from which all military salutes are fired, and the Arsenal Yard are on the left shortly after passing the Naval Yard. Chinese houses and shops of an ordinary type follow and in a mile and a quarter the entrance to the Naval Hospital is reached. The hospital, with quarters for the medical staff, is built on the summit of the hill called Mount Shadwell. A short ascent brings one to Morrison Hill, the road here being a steep cutting through the hill, then straight down the other side of the hill into the Wongneichung Valley—generally known as the Happy Valley. Running round the foot of the valley is the Race-course, training ground, and Grand Stand belonging to the Hongkong Jockey Club. The annual races are held during the third week in February. The whole Colony makes holiday on the race days and then the Happy Valley is thronged with all classes and all nations on racing pleasure bent. The course is nearly a mile round and the races are run with China ponies. During the winter months the training of the ponies takes place, principally in the early morning, when they may be seen taking their exercises by the side of the course or along the valley.

The China pony is bred in the Far North, on the Mongolian plains, and when he is about five to six years old he is brought down to the Treaty ports—mostly to Shanghai—for sale. He is then very much in the rough and to look at is not at all a sightly nag. In shape he is a horse on short legs, long and low, a plain head, rather short neck, straight shoulders, and a long back; he has, however, plenty of bone, a good deal of depth, and generally good legs, his height varies from 12 ft. 3 in. to 14 hands, but the 13 hand and 13. 1 ponies are decidedly the best shaped. When you first get on him you at once have a feeling there is nothing in front of you, and, as he carries his head low, especially in the gallop, you feel the reverse of comfortable until you get used to him. With his native owners he shows a very docile disposition, but usually has a very different way of treating a foreign master until he becomes accustomed to him. He can never be thoroughly trusted, however, for he resembles his human compatriot for treachery, and, after appearing to be perfectly under control, will suddenly develop some of his original instincts.

He has a mouth of iron and will often take charge of you, but has a most wonderful knack of escaping collision, he has a great objection to hurting himself and will pull up dead rather than run into anything. If you wish to test your seat you can find plenty of buck jumpers among his species, but rearing is an accomplishment he does not thoroughly understand. As a racer he is wonderfully good for his size, carrying heavy weights, between 11 and 12 stone, over $1\frac{1}{2}$ mile to 2 mile courses. If you get one of the right sort, he is a good plucked one and will struggle and stand hard riding for the last $\frac{1}{2}$ or $\frac{3}{4}$ of a mile of a long race in the most determined manner. His action in trotting is not good, rather the daisy cutter style, and he is not at all a showy trap pony. He perhaps shows to the greatest advantage across country, going up or down the most impossible looking banks, sometimes almost perpendicular, with the greatest ease, and if you trust to him he will rarely bring you to grief. Weight affects him but little, and it is often astonishing during a drag or paper hunt to see the game little fellow carrying a 12 or 13 stone man for a 10 or 12 mile gallop over about the roughest imaginable going, and taking jumps every few hundred yards, sometimes clearing as much as 12 to 15 feet of water. In former days English and Australian horses used to run in the races, but the custom has died out in favour of the China ponies.

On the western side of the valley are the cemeteries. The first, nearest Morrison Hill Road, is the Mohammedan cemetery, then the Roman Catholic, Anglican, Parsee and Hindoo cemeteries. The Anglican cemetery is beautifully laid out with walks amidst trees and flowers. At the end of the valley, where the hills begin to close in, is the native village of Wongneichung. This village is much the same now as it was 200 years ago and is a good specimen of the native villages of southern China, built with narrow streets and passages to ensure against surprise from the outer world. The tall lychee trees to the south-east of the village will be admired. They were planted when the village was built and were cultivated for the market. The trees, however, no longer bear any fruit. Following the road on the western side of the village a stone pathway leading to the Jews' cemetery is reached.

Near this neglected cemetery is the site of what used to be called the Haunted House and is now a favourite place for picnics. The *real* Haunted House, was not here at all, however, but on the hills east of the valley. It was so called because three partners of Messrs. Jardine, Matheson & Co. died there within eighteen months. It was haunted by fever. For those who have not an extra hour to spare this part of the excursion may be omitted.

The Stanley Road, which we must follow to Taitam, follows between the race-course and the village and, turning to the right on the eastern side of the village, the steep ascent to Wongneichung Gap commences. Some parts of this road are very pretty, but some portions are steep and uninteresting. On the way up from the valley a huge black rock is passed, the traditional first halting place of picnic parties, then Bowen Road (right) and the western end of the Taitam tunnel (left) are reached. This end of the tunnel and the embankment across the ravine are fine pieces of work. The water flows out of the tunnel into a conduit leading direct to the filtering beds and service reservoir above Garden Road. It is the roof of this long conduit which forms the foundation of the Bowen Road above which is now one of the principal and most interesting walks in the island. Not very far above this the road to Taitam turns to the left, and the road to Little Hongkong, Aberdeen, Pokfulam and so home to the city, branches off through a deep cutting on the right. The road to Taitam need rise no higher than this, but it does, and crosses the ridge at a point much higher than necessary. After toiling over this ridge and meeting with the wildest and most lovely scenery the island affords, the road rapidly descends through treeless valleys to the great Taitam reservoir and the other end of the tunnel. Some time may be spent here in examining the reservoir and the big dam.

Passing on down along the stream curving from the reservoir, the pretty wooded village of Taitam Tuk is reached. Here is the head of Taitam Bay, and on a May day, when the hillsides are covered with flowers, chiefly those of the wild myrtle, few more delightful scenes can be imagined. The return journey can be made from here along the Bowen Road direct or by the longer route through Little Hongkong and the road round the south-western side of the island.

If the visitor has further time to spare he may go on to Stanley and take the road from there to Little Hongkong. From Taitam to Stanley is about two miles. The road follows the picturesque coast and over precipitous cliffs upon which the sea breaks. Stanley was the site of the military cantonment in the early days of the Colony. In its little cemetery there are grave stones dated in 1841, the year when the island was ceded.

Stanley was abandoned by the military authorities as unhealthy, but it may be questioned whether it really need have been so regarded. The water is brackish, but although there is an unfailing supply of excellent water within about a mile, they did nothing to bring it in. That they never planted a tree is a matter of course, military ground never does grow anything but a crop of ugly stones marked " W.D." If Stanley were planted and supplied with water, and its foreshore reclaimed where necessary, it would make a charming watering place, with delightful sea-bathing and all the attractions of Macao, except of course the gambling houses, which are the only attraction to the *canaille* that go there. A canal, only a few yards in length, cut between the two bays, would enable junks to anchor in either without beating round a long headland, and would thus provide a secure anchorage in either monsoon. At present Stanley Harbour is thronged in winter and deserted in summer. There is a place behind the point which forms the western side of the harbour where a steamer from Victoria might land passengers without going round Stanley point, where it is apt to be a little rough at times, and a slight cutting through the hill would enable them to walk in on the level and the road to town might be shortened by two miles.

About a mile and a half beyond Stanley is a curious little village called Wong-ma Kok. It is a charming spot for a picnic, but no picnic party need attempt to find it without a guide, for it lies in a wooded and cup-like hollow on the top of a hill, and is invisible from everywhere. Moreover a steam-launch to return from Stanley in, is an essential to a successful picnic at Wong-ma Kok, for twenty miles steady walking is too much to get out of a party within the day.

This village was once occupied by a band of pirates, who had their own gunpowder mill there, and, so entirely secluded is the place that for years the Government did not suspect its existence, nor were the inhabitants called upon to pay taxes, for the simple reason that the tax-gatherers had never found out they were there. But this mountain fastness was adorned with its own Lorna Doone, and her *beaux yeux* brought its history to a close in a very tragic manner. There was a Chinese damsel there more attractive, or less unattractive, than the ordinary run of native girls to be found in a fishing village, Although the collectors of taxes did not know the way to Wong-ma Kok, Captain da Costa, stationed at Stanley, did know it, and climbed the rocky path but too often. Captain da Costa had come into some property, he was to leave for England the next day, his brother officers had given him a farewell feast, after which, with a comrade,

"Being full of supper and distempering draughts,"

he set out for one more visit to the secret bower he had discovered. What took place there nobody ever knew exactly, but next day, neither of the officers having returned, an alarm was raised, somebody volunteered to show the way to the village, it was found to be utterly deserted, there were marks of a severe struggle, a trail of blood led down to the beach, and neither of the officers was ever seen again alive. The body of one was recovered under circumstances which read like a page from a sensation novel. A whole day had been spent searching for the bodies in recesses of the rocky shore without success. It was getting dark, and the officer in charge of the police boat gave the order to return, feeling that further search was useless. As they pushed off from the rocks, a Chinese dropped his boat-hook overboard, and it disappeared in a thick mass of sea-weed, in which he groped for it. "Never mind the boat-hook, give way," said the officer, but the man still went on searching for it, when the hand of the murdered man came up through the weed, as if beckoning for assistance. The other body it was afterwards ascertained had been sunk out at sea. One of the chief pirates afterwards fell into the hands of the Government, and, whilst awaiting his trial for the murder, he committed suicide, in prison.

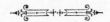

CHAPTER IX.

The Roads and Streets of Victoria, and the Neighbourhood.—
The Botanic Gardens.

THE roads and streets of the City are necessarily adapted to the steep and varying slopes of the hill sides and the comparatively narrow strip of flat land between the harbour and the foot of the hills, a great deal of which has been reclaimed from the sea. The city of Victoria is in length from East to West a little over four miles, but its breadth from North to South varies from half a mile for the central portions to two or three hundred yards in the eastern and western portions.

The Praya is a fine road 50 feet wide, running along the whole front of the City except where the Military Barracks and Naval Yard divide the City into two portions. The road is protected on the harbour side by a strong retaining wall of faced granite, made level with the road itself. Along the Praya, facing the harbour, are the houses of business and storehouses (or godowns) of merchants, shippers and traders, and jutting into the harbour from the other side of the Praya are numerous wharves, some public, of which Pedder's Wharf is the principal, and the rest, the private property of steamship companies or merchants.

The first wharf, going westward, from Pedder's Wharf is that of the Douglas Steamship Company, Limited, whence start the Company's steamers for the Coast Ports and the Island of Formosa. A few hundred yards further is the wharf of the

China Navigation Company, whence their splendid river steamer, the *Hankow*, leaves every other day for Canton, and a little further on is the wharf of the Hongkong, Canton, and Macao Steamboat Company, Limited, whose magnificent river steamers leave daily for Canton and Macao. The other wharves along the Praya are used chiefly by steam-launches and by junks and boats for landing cargo into the godowns. The Praya is divided into Praya Central, Praya West and Praya East. Praya Central commences at the harbour side of the City Hall and extends to the Harbour Office, a distance of nearly a mile. Praya West commences at the Harbour Office and extends to West Point and Kennedy Town at the extreme West of the City. Praya East commences at the Arsenal Yard beyond the Military Barracks and Naval Yard and extends to East Point.

Queen's Road.—This is the principal street and runs the whole length of the City for four miles parallel to the Praya at a distance of a hundred yards from it. Here are the houses of the Banking and other Companies, the Hongkong Club, the offices of professional gentlemen, and the magazines of the principal storekeepers and traders. The European houses occupy the central portion only; the whole of the western and eastern districts, except where the Military Barracks, Naval Yard and Arsenal are located, being occupied by Chinese shops of every description.

Wyndham Street, leading up from Queen's Road Central by the eastern side of the Hongkong Club to Glenealy, is the literary street of the Colony. The offices of the "China Mail" newspaper are on the right hand side ascending from Queen's Road at the corner of the upper side of Wellington Street, which commences here. Opposite is the handsome building of the Club Germania, and a little higher on the right, just before the road winds to the right, with Lower Albert Road to the left, and the beautiful rockery of Glenealy in front, are the offices of the " Daily Press " the morning newspaper of the Colony.   The buildings on the left are known as Pedder's Hill where is located the " Hongkong Telegraph," one of the evening newspapers.   The Dairy Farm Company, Limited, has its town offices, distributing centre, and refreshment rooms in the neat building opposite the " Daily Press " Office.

Glenealy commences at the top of Wyndham Street and crossing Caine Road leads into the Robinson Road, which runs from East to West along the higher confines of the City. Glenealy is very beautiful from the rockeries where grow trees, ferns, bushes, and choice shrubs luxuriantly.   From the upper part of Glenealy are entrances into the Botanic Garden.

Caine Road leads from Glenealy through the higher levels of the City to Bonham Road, which is really a continuation of Caine Road, into the Pokfulam Road.   Near the commencement of Caine Road is the Roman Catholic Cathedral, and the residences of many merchants, professional and business men are situated in this road in which are also the Italian Convent and Spanish Procuration.   Not thirty years ago Caine Road was the highest road in the Victoria.   Near the commencement of Bonham Road are the mission and other residential buildings of the London Missionary Society.

Robinson Road is above the Caine Road at a level of about 300 feet above the sea.   It leads from the Peak Road to the Upper Richmond ,Road and the western part of Bonham Road and so on to the Pokfulam Road.   It is now the highest road running East and West in the City.   The herbarium and offices of the Superintendent of the Botanic and Afforestation Department are situated at the East end of Robinson Road.   St. Joseph's College and several gentlemen's private residences are along this road.

Garden Road leads from the Queen's Road between the Parade Ground and Murray Barracks, past St. John's Cathedral, then the lower terminus of the Tramway called St. John's Place, and up a long steep incline along the eastern boundary of the Botanic Gardens and past St. Joseph's Church to the commencement of the Bowen Road, and here turning to the right into the Peak Road where Robinson Road commences. The Upper Albert Road leads out of Garden Road to the principal entrance of the Botanic Gardens (left), Government House and grounds (right), and on to Glenealy where Caine Road commences.

Kennedy Road takes its start in an easterly direction from Garden Road opposite the lower part of the Botanic Gardens and near St. Joseph's Church. Crossing by bridges over the ravine and Tramway line, where there is a station, it passes the Union Church and parsonage and winds along for a considerable distance, following the contours of the hills to the hills above the district of Wanchai and the Naval Hospital, when it descends into the far end of Queen's Road East near the Gap at Morrison Hill. About half way it passes just above the military magazine, the ravine there leading up to Magazine Gap, but there is no pathway. The next ravine, about half a mile further along the road, leads up to Wanchai Gap; here there is a steep bit of road leading up to Wanchai Gap and down the other side to the village of Aberdeen, where it joins the road along the southside of the Island. Kennedy Road is so named after the late Governor, Sir Arthur Kennedy, and ten years ago was the fashionable Sunday evening walk in the Colony. The road is about a mile and a half long, for the most part about 150 feet above the sea level, and winding in and out of the ravines and overlooking the harbour has many attractions.

Bowen Road, named after Governor Sir George Bowen, commences at the upper part of the Garden Road, and, taking an easterly direction, leads into the Stanley Road high above the village of Wongnaichung. This road, including its windings, is about four miles long and is a level road the whole way from near its commencement.

Near the commencement is the Bowen Road Station on the Tramway line and the entrance to the filtering beds and service reservoir of the great Taitam water supply. The road is here about 350 feet above sea level and underneath is the conduit leading from the Stanley Road end of the Taitam tunnel to the filtering beds. This road is one of the favourite walks of the Colony. The views of the successive ravines obtained in walking along this road are extremely beautiful, and from its altitude the scenery over the harbour and of the mainland mountains is also very fine.

Magazine Gap Road starts from the Bowen Road, a short distance past the bridge over the tramway line, and leads obliquely up the hills, with a moderately gentle ascent to Magazine Gap, at an altitude of 900 feet above sea level. Here the view extends, on the northern side, over the harbour and the mainland, and, on the southern side, over the China Sea to the Lema Islands and the Asses Ears, an island with a double peak twenty-three miles south. Several gentlemen's residences have been erected near Magazine Gap, principally on the southern side. From Magazine Gap the road continues to ascend gradually, and passing under the abrupt cliffs of Mount Gough, leads into Plantation Road and the Peak district at an altitude of about 1,200 feet above sea level. The Magazine Gap Road is also a favorite walk from the City to the Peak district, and many prefer to ride up by tram to Victoria Gap and walk back to the City by the Plantation and Magazine Gap Roads, these roads commanding beautiful views at every turn.

The Peak Road starts from the Upper Albert Road, near its junction with Glenealy and Caine Road, and ascends between the Botanic Gardens to the Albany and Robinson Roads (altitude 300 feet). Continuing its ascent, the tennis courts of the Ladies' Recreation Club are reached (altitude 400 feet) and a little higher on the right is the entrance to Queen's Gardens (altitude 500 feet); above Queen's Gardens are a few more picturesque residential houses and then a steep ascent into the hills above ; then Plantation Road to the left and winding up to the right from Plantation Road is Victoria Gap (altitude 1,250 feet) before described.

A few years ago the Peak Road used to be the only means of direct access to the Peak and the climb on foot was tiresome and uninteresting until an altitude of 1,000 feet was reached, and few were the people who ventured the ascent without a four coolie chair. Now, by means of the Peak Tramway, the ascent is easy and interesting and the Peak Road for a walk in now only taken by those who prefer to take their "constitutional" in a stiff sharp ascent.

Pokfulam Road.—Starts from Queen's Road West opposite the Sailors Home and winding up the hill passes the end of Bonham Road, and then still leading upward, passes between a spur of Victoria Peak and Mount Davis. The old Chinese cemetery, now closed, is on the northern side of Mount Davis and the Chinese protestant cemetery is on the southern side   The road then winds round the hill sides to the southern side of the island until the village of Pokfulam is reached.   Here is the farm of the Dairy Farm Company, Limited, the Sanitarium of the French Mission, a few gentlemen's residences, a Police Station and a small Chinese village.   A path on the left hand side by the Police Station leads up the hill to the Pokfulam reservoir, which until a few years ago was the sole source of water supply to the

City, but is now an auxiliary to the Taitam water supply. This path continues up the mountain side to Victoria Gap. Returning to Pokfulam, the main road continuing in an easterly direction descends a long and steep hill to the beach and the village of Aberdeen. At the commencement of the village are the Aberdeen Docks of the Hongkong and Whampoa Dock Company, Limited, and at the other end are the Paper Mills belonging to a private company. Here by the courtesy of the manager, may be seen the process of manufacture of Chinese paper by the newest and most improved English machinery. The road continues to the village of Little Hongkong, where is the largest forest on the Island; it then winds from Little Hongkong to the village of Stanley, or by a road leading out of it to the left soon after leaving Little Hongkong, to the Wongnaichung Gap, and so home by the Bowen Road or the Happy Valley before described.

The Botanic Gardens.—The Botanic Gardens are splendidly situated on rising ground between the Upper Albert Road and the Albany and Robinson Roads, and cover an extensive area. They are under the charge of the Botanical and Afforestation Department, of which Mr. Charles Ford, F.L.S., is the Superintendent. Many a spare hour may be profitably spent in wandering along the beautiful walks and terraces in which these gardens are laid out. Their close proximity to the City renders them a favorite resort for all classes of the community. Here grow in native beauty all kinds of tropical and sub-tropical trees from all the warm countries of the world. The following is a selection of the most interesting trees growing in these gardens and, as the names of all are placed on or near the trees, the visitor will have little difficulty in identifying them :—

NATIVE TREES.

i.e. *Natives of China and Hongkong.*

Rhodoleia Championi.—Ornamental flowers; known from Hongkong only.

Spathodea cauda-felinæ.—Catstail-like seed pods.

Magnolia conspicua.—Large white flowers.

Symplocos decora.—Lovely sweet-scented flowers.

Heteropanax fragrans.—Ornamental dark green foliage.

Stittingia sebifera.—The tallow tree.

Cratæva religiosa.—Ornamental cream-coloured flowers.

Murraza exotica.—Sweet-scented white flowers.

Quercus salicina.—Willow-leaved oak.

Viburnum odoratissimum.—Ornamental red berries.

Cinnamomum cassia.—The cassia-bark tree.

Illicium verum.—True star-anise.

FOREIGN TREES.

Alemites triloba.—Candle-nut from Molluccas.

Ficus macrophylla.—Moreton Bay fig.

Ficus elastica.—India-rubber tree.

Melaleuca leucadendron.—Cajuputi oil tree from Australia.

Plumieria acuminata.—Frangipani, sweet-scented flowers.

Michelia champaca.—Sweet-scented flowers.

Magnolia grandiflora.—Handsome tree with large sweet flowers from U.S

Cassia fistula.—The pudding-pipe tree of India.

Grevillea robusta.—Australian " Silky-oak."

Albizzia Lebbek.—Large shade tree.

Cinnamomum Zeylanaum.—The Ceylon cinnamon.

Bixa Orellana.—The Arnotta dye tree.

Artocarpus integrifolius.—The Jack-fruit.

Ilex paraguayensis.—The Maté-tea tree of South America.

Tamarindus indicus.—Tamarind tree.

Haematoxylon campechianum.—The logwood tree.

CONIFERS.

Cupressus funebris.—Funereal cypress of China.

Cupressus Tornlosa.—Himalayan cypress.

Cedrus Deodara.—Himalayan deodar.

Cryptomaria japonica.

Callitris rhomboidea.—A lovely tree from Queensland.

Taxodium distichum.—Deciduous cypress.

Arancaria excelsa.—Norfold Island pine.

Arancaria Cunninghamii.—Queensland pine.

Arancaria Bidwillii.—Bunza Bunza from Queensland.

PALMS.

Livistona Chinensis.—Chinese fan palm.

Livistona Australis.—Australian fan palm.

Archontophoenix Alexandrae.—Handsome species of tall palm from Queensland.

Orcxdoxa oleracea.—Cabbage palm.

Orcxdoxa regia.

Phoenix dactylifera.—Date palm.

Cocos nucifera.—Cocoa-nut.

Arenga sacchan'fera.—Sugar palm.

Rhapis flabelliformis.—Ground rattan of China and Japan.

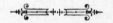

CHAPTER X.

RUNNING as it does obliquely right across the Island, the Stanley Road naturally forms the basis for a good many walks, but they are all of some length and require at least a whole afternoon. Not far from the highest point of the road, a deep cutting leads off to the right into that to *Little Hongkong*, as the residents here persist in calling a pretty little village, mainly because that is not its name. For some distance after leaving the Stanley Road the way is over singularly bare and bleak hills, but it suddenly turns into a wooded valley, and the last mile is as pretty as could be desired.

Some years ago Little Hongkong was the one place to which Big Hongkong had any idea of going for a picnic. A house had been built there for picnic purposes in the very old days of the Colony, and was somewhat fitfully maintained by subscriptions. There was no made track after leaving the Stanley Road, and persons who did a couple of miles of hill scrambling before eating a tremendous meal at Hongkong village (that is what the Chinese call it) thought they had done something of distinguished difficulty. Some, *horresco referens*, were carried out in chairs the whole distance, by way of Pokfulum and Aberdeen, ate their portentous meal, and were carried all the way back again. We have changed all that, or a great deal of it. Little Hongkong became so hopelessly vulgarised by these feeds of the benighted rich that few people who want really to enjoy a picnic care to go there. A house is very well adapted to setting out the Persian apparatus, but as plainer living (and, let us hope, higher thinking) became the rule, few people cared to have the Persian apparatus at picnics, and even its splendour did not redeem the discomfort of lunching surrounded by a whining and obtrusive crowd, no more to be driven away than the flies which are another unpleasant local peculiarity. Moreover when there was a cut road made the whole way, going to Little Hongkong became a very tame affair. People discovered, to their surprise, that there are lots of other places to go to, that a house is by no means a necessity, that a huge meal spoils more pleasure than it gives, and Little Hongkong fell into not undeserved neglect. The house is now in ruins. People who still go there tiffin in the woods-Whilst at Little Hongkong, a stroll down to the beach is worth taking. It is a boulder beach and the sea is particularly clear and pure there.

When Little Hongkong was the one place to which every. body went for picnics there were keen controversies about the best way to get there. Daring spirits advocated a certain by-path over what is called the Cemetery Gap, and something like a paper war raged in the visitors' book kept at the little bungalow. To go by the Cemetery Gap, it is necessary to enter the Anglican Cemetery and strike up a spur of the hill to the left. This leads by a charming mountain path, to a pass directly overlooking Little Hongkong, and the descent is pretty as well as the ascent. Even this is not the very shortest way. That must be found by going to the stone bridge at the far end of the Happy Valley, and taking a path up through the wood to the right, a path almost as steep as a ladder. The Cemetery Gap way to Little Hongkong is doubtless much shorter than the other, but it should only be attempted by young people who are good walkers, on a cold day when there is little sun. A hot sun on your back all the way up a steep hill-side is very trying. The top of the steep hill overlooking the Happy Valley is easily reached from the Cemetery Gap, or Bowen Road, and commands a splendid view. By keeping along the ridge, it is possible to descend to the Stanley Road at the junction of the Little Hongkong Road, and so return home.

If the pedestrian, however, turns to the left before reaching the top of the pass, he may, under skilful guidance, find the famous *Rhodoleia Championi,* which grows in the wood not very far from the top of the rocky watercourse which is so conspicuous at the south-west corner of the Happy Valley. This beautiful tree has never been found growing anywhere else than in Hongkong, nor in Hongkong anywhere but here, though from this tree cuttings have been taken for the Botanic Gardens, and for all parts of the world. The explorer will certainly not find the *Rhodoleia* without a guide, he may not find it with one, but if he does succeed he will have no difficulty in following on the same contour of the hill, across the head of the watercourse mentioned, where there is a splendid view, and so coming down to the site of what used to be called the Haunted House, from which he can reach the Happy Valley.

Deep Bay.—Another excursion to be made from the Stanley Road is to Deep Bay. Turn off as if going to Little Hongkong, and then take the first rough track to the left. Both Deep Bay and the way down to it are prettier and more interesting than they appear when seen from the hillside above. The beach is a model one for bathing, smooth clean sand, which slopes sharply but evenly, and the sea, as pure as sapphire, comes in in little rollers. There was once a cavalry encampment at this spot, its lines can still be traced. The road round the Island runs just above the beach, and whether it is followed over the hill to Little Hongkong, or round the coast to Shallow Bay, it is very lovely just here, in fact it is one of the most charming parts of the Colony.

Shallow Water Bay.—One more walk before quitting the Stanley Road and we have done with it, but it is a walk of heroic length. Follow the road nearly to Tai-tam Tuk. A wide valley will be found opening on the right, and up this valley is a track. It can be followed, not without difficulty, until it leads over a saddle in the range of hills into Shallow-water Bay, where is perhaps the finest beach in the Island, of smooth white sand almost as firm as a pavement. From this beach a lovely bit of road leads into Deep Bay, and so home.

Causeway Bay.—Keeping eastward from the Happy Valley along the northern shore of the Island we come to Causeway Bay, the home of the Polo Club. In front of it is a harbour of refuge for boats in the typhoon season. In Causeway Bay are two curious temples, rather prettily situated, the further one of which—the Temple of the Queen of Heaven (Tin Hau)—is undoubtedly the most popular Chinese place of worship in the Island. It is worth while to pay a visit to this spot on the Chinese new year's day. The throng of gaily dressed and merry worshippers, and the array of stalls laden with light-coloured papers and candles for offerings form a scene more like an old English fair than any thing else. A good long walk is to be found even at Causeway Bay. Strike up the Bay towards the village, and ascend the valley behind it. It is both easy and pretty. On reaching the crest of the hill the whole Tai-tam valley lies open before you. Turn to the right and make a scramble for the Stanley Road. It is rather a rough scramble however.

Shau-ki Wan is a thriving little market town about seven miles from Victoria at the far end of the level Eastward Road.

To walk there and walk back is somewhat tedious, the best plan is to go by the steam-ferry from Victoria and walk home. If you are above sitting amongst Chinese for an hour, get the skipper of the steam ferry to tow your own boat if you have one, which he will do for a very moderate payment. The road to Shau-ki Wan was the Rotten Row of the Colony in those stupid days when every one thought himself bound to keep a carriage, whether he could afford it or not, and the sole amusement was solemnly driving along this weary road every afternoon! Those *were* stupid times, may they never return! There was no croquet, there was no lawn tennis. The man who walked over the hills was regarded as a lunatic, he who walked on the level as a pauper. There was no real pleasure, nothing but a heavy and pompous extravagance, with no return for the huge sums fooled away, an astounding ignorance of all the surroundings, the Chinese, their language and their ways, or even of the very place itself, and a great deal of insolence and the pride of life. The monuments of that dreary old time remain in the first and second turnings, as they were called, on the Shau-ki Wan Road, the third turning has been obliterated in recent years by the Sugar Refinery at Quarry Bay belonging to the Taikoo Sugar Refinery Company, Limited.

In Shau-ki Wan Harbour there is a tumble-down old temple perched on a rock. A former Governor of Hongkong once conceived the idea of building a Police Station upon the rock, and he sent out to the elders of the village to know what they would take for the Temple. They replied that the shrine was one of the oldest in the neighbourhood. It had been a holy place from time immemorial. If His Excellency wanted the rock it was of course at his disposition, but as to putting a money value on it, there were some things that money could not buy. The Temple remained undisturbed.

Shau-ki Wan forms a starting point for five very interesting walks, which are best commenced by going to this village by water, or driving there. They are (1) the ascent of Mount Parker, (2) Tai-tam Tuk, (3) Round the Island, (4) Shek-O, (5) Cape d'Aguilar. Cold days should be chosen for all these.

Mount Parker.—The ascent of Mount Parker is essentially one of those walks where you *must* know the path and stick to it. Nothing but fatigue and disappointment can result from attempts to invent a path of your own. The summit can be reached from Quarry Bay, or even from Causeway Bay, but the best way is to take the road from Shau-ki Wan to Tai-tam, and follow it to about its highest point. Here a well marked track will be found, to the right, near a bridge; follow that. Before the ridge is reached a charming spot will be found with level ground for arranging tiffin, and a spring of clear water. The ladies of the party will probably elect to remain here. On reaching the ridge keep along it to the top. The view is superb, especially over Mirs Bay, and from no point is so good a bird's-eye view of Hongkong obtainable. There are several summits, all about the same height. If nobody has been left behind at the tiffin place, it is possible to go home a different way by descending the ridge to the Gap above Quarry Bay, and then following a good path down from the Gap to the Shau-ki Wan Road at Quarry Bay.

Round the Island.—The made road round the eastern side of Mount Parker would have taken us, had we not left it, to Tai-tam Tuk, from whence we could have returned to town by the Stanley Road. This of itself forms a charming picnic route, and the same ground forms part of the vaunted walk round the Island, which, in all candour be it said, is really not a walk round the Island at all. There is no track even, much less a road all round the coast, and if there were, the distance would be from forty to fifty ·miles. By what is *called* round the Island it is only twenty-five, and will take seven hours good solid walking to accomplish.

This is the ordinary route, indeed there is no other (except by going the other way round)—from town to Shau-ki Wan, then across the hill by the made road above Sai Wan to Tai-tam Tuk. Here cross the estuary on the sands if the tide is ont. Go on to Stanley, turn to the right, cross into Shallow Bay, then into Deep Bay, then Little Hongkong, Aberdeen, Pokfulum, and home. There is now a fairly good road the whole way, and hardly an uninteresting bit in it.

If one wants to discover that he has been very far from really going round the Island, he has only to make a subsequent expedition (by the same road) to Shek-O or Cape d'Aguilar. The made road to Shek-O has somewhat taken the beauty out of the walk. There used to be no way there but by descending into Sai-wan past the ruins of the old barracks, and climbing up through the woods on the other side to the Gap which overlooks Shek-O. You can still go this way, it takes just as long as the easier but much more circuitous road. When the conspicuous gap south of Sai-wan is reached there is nothing more to do but to "follow your nose." Shek-O is not in itself a pretty place, but the coast before you come to it is extremely pretty, and so are the green downs (if one may venture so to call them) over which the road leads. The great charm of the whole district, however, is the way the sea comes in from the Pacific Ocean to the secluded little bays, in long rollers, the like of which cannot be seen elsewhere in the island.

About two miles beyond Shek-O, along the same road, Cape d'Aguilar is reached, and a very long tramp it is. A steam launch is the best means of getting there if a little rolling is not a fatal objection. For it is almost impossible to reach Cape

H

d'Aguilar by water, whichever way you go round, without some motion, probably a good deal, and this generally so effectually spoils the pleasure of the day for 'ladies that it is perhaps better to select some other place.   It is rather selfish of men who are not afraid of sea-sickness to persuade ladies (who, of course, believe them) that "there won't be any motion to speak of."   That is generally true, because the victims are much too ill to speak of it.   The sea is very seldom smooth off Cape d'Aguilar and when the wind comes down even in half a gale from the north-east, the rollers soon become lashed up into furious waves.

When you are at the Cape however it is a strikingly pretty place, the coast is fine, the view is magnificent, and the air is exhilarating.   There is the lighthouse to see, and some curious caves, into which the sea rolls, and which on a really rough day must be an awful sight.

Taimoshan.—The excursion, however, which may be regarded as the pilgrimage to Mecca for all faithful pedestrians is the ascent of Tai-mo Shan on the mainland opposite Hongkong. This massive hill, nearly 4,000 feet high, is almost in the centre of the indented peninsula which forms the San On district, the political division of China which lies nearest to us, and of which Kowloon city is the capital.   Looking across the harbour nearly due north it cannot fail to attract the eye, if the top be not wrapped in clouds, as it often is.   An expedition to Tai-mo Shan (*Great Watchtower Mountain*, so called probably from its being formerly used as a military watch tower) should start not later than eight in the morning, and have steam as far as Tsün Wàn, the village in a deep bay behind Stonecutter's Island. From here there is only one way to the summit, but as no two members of the Hongkong Alpine Club agree upon which way that is, it is as well not to go into details about it, especially as they would be wholly useless.   One may possibly be allowed to mention his modest but unalterable conviction that his way is *the* way, and that there is no other, and his utter scepticism as to statements about a path "almost to the top," unless almost means at least six or seven hundred feet. And that last pull is, it must be confessed, a very stiff one, whether the grass be long and thus hide all the big stones, or whether it has just been burned, and so all the ground be slippery with black ashes which rise up and choke you.

The chief attraction at the top is a hole, some two or three feet deep, into which each tired mountaineer, one straggling up after another, tumbles, to the unconcealed delight of those who have been up before, and, even knowing all about it, have not improbably tumbled in again. Whether it is worth while to toil up so far to enjoy this small practical joke may be a question, but I am bound to admit I have never seen much of a view from Tai-mo Shan. There must be a magnificent view sometimes, but the Hongkong pedestrian necessarily arrives there in the middle of a winter's day, when very little is visible but haze and glare. There is no way back but the way you came. The best place for tiffin is a sort of shoulder, about 600 feet below the summit. Go to the top first, you certainly won't go afterwards. An Alpen-stock is useful on this walk, and so are neutral tinted goggles, a pair of which is an immense comfort on any midday excursion. A few rare ferns are found near the top of Tai-mo Shan, of which one has never been discovered elsewhere except in Java.

This big hill stands in the middle of a good deal of very green and pretty country. There is a freshness and verdure about it which we do not see in Hongkong, still less in the abominably barren and gnarled hills opposite, with their dreary foreshores. A good deal of this pleasing district is taken up with pine-apple cultivation, and several charming walks can be made to terminate at Tsün Wàn aforesaid, from which place it is better to have steam to return with. Of these walks the chief and crown is that to the *Sandal Wood Mill*, perhaps the prettiest walk but one in this neighbourhood, and certainly the most difficult to find. Let no party venture without a guide who, in addition to saying he knows the way, really knows it. Most people take this walk wrong end first. They go to Tsün Wàn, find their way to the mill (or to *a* mill, for they often hit on the wrong one) and then walk back to the shore opposite Hongkong near the Cosmopolitan Dock. The result is that you have all the hard work after tiffin, and an interminable pull up hill with the afternoon sun in your eyes. Instead of this blunder, start not later than 10, land on the shore above the Dock (giving a wide berth to any boats you may see inshore there, for the spicy breezes blow uncommonly strong from them) walk over the hills to the mill, and tiffin there. All your hard work is done before tiffin, and with the sun at your back. After that you have only a pleasant down-hill walk to Tsün Wàn, where let us hope a cup of tea awaits you. The immediate neighbourhood of the mill is simply charming, only it is rather difficult (and in a wooded country too) to find a shady place for tiffin. A light tent, which two coolies can carry, is an immense addition to the comfort of any picnic party, and is to be recommended much more than an equal weight of champagne. It shields equally from wind or sun, and serves for another day, which the champagne doesn't.

A shorter but very pleasing walk in this neighbourhood is taken by landing at what is called American Town, behind Stonecutters' Island, crossing the hill to Gin-drinkers' Bay (which is prettier than its name) and so to Tsün Wàn.

When we climbed over the hill from the Cosmopolitan Docks, we reached, at the top of the first ascent, a grassy pass from which we descended again into an inland valley. But if, instead of descending, we had turned sharp to the right, keeping for a time on the level, we should gradually have come down into a wooded valley which lies behind the precipitous hill known as the Lion's Head. From this valley the reason of the name becomes apparent, the rocks on the top of that hill, seen from the north form a colossal lion, as life-like every bit, as Sir Edwin Landseer's lions in Trafalgar Square. Half-way up the hill is another curious rock, embossomed in trees. It is exactly like a Chinese woman with a baby strapped on her back. The figure must be fifty feet high, and the resemblance is curiously perfect. From this pretty valley two good paved roads lead over the hill, one east, one west of the Lion's head—good, that is to say, till the summit is reached, after which, down to Kowloon city, all is barrenness, desolation, and decay. Climbing up these really well-made roads, evidently centuries old, with not a stone started, it is difficult to carry the mind back to a time when, in this remotest corner of China, there were public works, organisation, and some sort of settled government. Yet that such a time there was, the fortifications, such as they are, of Kowloon city are witnesses.

This curious and particularly dirty little Kowloon city occupies an exact parallelogram, but as usual there are more suburbs than city. The circuit of the walls can be made in five minutes. The formalities usually insisted upon in garrison towns as to permits, &c., are dispensed with here. Nobody requests you to pass and give the countersign. You come, you see, you walk round. The cannon on the walls suggest the idea that you would rather be a good way off when any attempt is made to fire them. One or two petty officers are stationed on this dreary spot, and they must have a dull time of it. The chief trade of the place is from the several gambling houses erected near the beach there.

It is a mistake to ascend the Lion's Head from the Hongkong side.   The walk across the Kowloon peninsula is interesting, but the steep climb under a mid-day sun is simply suffocating.   Get to the *other* side of the hills, where are the green and pleasant spots, and if possible get there by water.

Visitors to Hongkong will probably hear of a place with the mysterious name *Malatoon*, and may possibly wonder what language this extraordinary word belongs to.   Ma-lau Tung (that is its real name [*]) is on the ridge of the hill about two miles east of the Lion's Head, and a very pretty spot it is, though the average Hongkong picnic party goes to it the worst way, up a bare and baking ravine, tiffins in the worst spot, and comes back the worst way, *i.e.* the way they went, with the afternoon sun in their eyes.   There is a more excellent way, if you have steam. Go outside the Lymun Pass and turn to the left into what is called Junk Bay.   Land on a green headland just before a sharp turn to the left.   Send your launch to the little block of houses opposite to wait for you.   From this headland a perfectly beautiful wooded track leads gently up, through charming country to Ma-lau Tung, where there is a much nicer and quieter place for tiffin than the one ordinarily selected.   After tiffin come down the southern face of the hill, also by a pretty track, to the bay where you left your launch.   You landed on the south side of it, you embark on the north.   A gig in tow is a necessity for the expedition.

The bay in which you now are is a centre of lovely walks. From this bay over to Kowloon city (taking Ma-lau Tung on the way if you like) is as pretty a walk as any in the neighbourhood.   But southward of this again is one, also said to end at Kowloon city, which would probably be found to run hard

---

* The name means Monkey Pond.   The chief reason for its being called so is because there are no ponds and no monkeys there.

the vaunted Sandal-wood mill. Here in a lovely afternoon in December it really involves no stretch of the imagination to fancy, for a few too brief minutes, that we are on an English cover-side,

> And Autumn laying here and there
> A fiery finger on the leaves.

Not the least charm of this particular district is the well-kept fields, which, when they are ploughed up in the dry season, look very like the fields at home. Only one thing is wanting, the cry of the rooks in the evening stillness, and that is a sound one does not hear in exile.

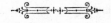

CHAPTER XI.

Meteorology and Climate—Sanitation—Flora and Fauna.

METEOROLOGY AND CLIMATE.

THE climate of Hongkong is greatly influenced by those periodical winds known as monsoons, as well as by its position immediately west of the great Pacific ocean, and its close proximity to the mountainous South eastern position of the continent of Asia, of which it practically forms part.— The climate comprises the two extremes of humidity and dryness. The mean temperature of the year is 72°. In January and February, the coolest months in the year, the temperature is 60°. The lowest reading varies in different years, and seldom falls below 42° at sea level, although in January, 1893, it was as low as 32°. The warmest months are from the end of May to the beginning of October, when the mean temperature is steady between 81° and 83°. The thermometer varies little from day to day, during the summer months, and the nights are nearly as hot as the days.

In the South West monsoon, which lasts from the end of May, to the beginning of October, the air is extremely humid, and total saturation will prevail for days together. From November to May, the period of the North East monsoon, the air is generally very dry, particularly in the months of November and December and the first two weeks of January, the mean humidity rarely exceeding 40 per cent of saturation, and frequently being less than 30. From October to the middle of January, the skies are generally very clear and the rainfall slight, the average not exceeding eight-tenths of an inch either in November, December, or January.

In July and August the rainfall is heaviest, the average being over 15 inches for each of those months, or nearly 31 inches for the two months. The wet months are the five months from May to September inclusive, during which nearly 70 inches of rain is received. The heaviest rainfall is during the thunderstorms which are frequent at the commencement of the South-west monsoon. In some of those storms the rain will fall at the rate of 3 inches an hour for two or three hours together. The mean rainfall for the year is 85 inches, distributed over 160 rainy days. The greatest fall in any one year of recent years was 120 inches in 1889, and the least 67 inches in 1887. The prevailing wind for eight months in the year, from September to April, is East. From May to August the prevailing wind is seldom the same two years together, but is mostly from South, South-west, or West. The month of September is the month when typhoons or cyclones are likely to pass over Hongkong. The last great typhoon, which is still remembered for its great destruction, happened during the night of the 22nd-23rd September 1874.

SANITATION.

Although Hongkong has only been British soil for fifty-two years, and although the now populous town of Victoria has entirely grown up during that comparatively short period, yet strange to relate, up to the year 1883, the sanitary condition of this most modern town was very indifferent indeed. Since 1883, a great many costly improvements have been carried out, and many are now in progress. Prior to 1883, the sanitation of the Colony was in the hands of the Colonial Engineer and the Colonial Surgeon. Owing to the frequent changes which took place in the incumbents of these two offices, there was no continuity of action in the sanitary administration of the Colony. Each new incumbent appears to have at once set to work to remedy what appeared to him to be the defects in the administration of his predecessor. The result was, (what such a system of administration must necessarily create) confusion.

In 1879, Sir John Pope Hennessy, then Governor of the Colony, seeing the confusion that existed, endeavoured to remedy it, and, as a first result of this interference with the working of the Public Works and Medical Departments, very serious differences arose between the Governor and the Heads of these Departments. In consequence of these differences in 1882, the Secretary of State for the Colonies sent out, at the Colony's expense, a special commissioner—Mr. Osbert Chadwick, C.M.G.—to enquire into and report on the sanitary condition of the Colony. Mr. Chadwick's report led to the establishment, in 1883, of a Sanitary Board, and the passing of a short Ordinance to enable this Board to at once carry out the more pressing of the many sanitary improvements which were pointed out in the report as being urgently required. This Board was re-constituted by Ordinance 24 of 1887. It is composed of four Members of the Civil Service of the Colony, two Members elected every three years by the ratepayers, and four Members appointed by the Governor, two of whom must be Chinese. The Board has a fairly complete staff with which to carry on its work, and such progress has been made that Victoria may now be fairly regarded as the cleanest town east of the Suez Canal and it will compare, as a whole, favourably with towns of similar size in England.

The water supply is of excellent quality and plentiful in summer, but not nearly sufficiently plentiful at the end of a long dry season to meet the requirements of the increasing population. The gathering grounds for the storage reservoirs are of granitic formation, and the quantity of vegetation on these grounds is comparatively little.

The main drainage of the European quarter of the town is good, and that of the Chinese quarter is rapidly being put into the same state. The drainage arrangements of the houses erected during the last four years are good, and the drains of many of the older houses have recently been put in excellent order, but a very great many houses are still, to say the least, very indifferently drained.

The surface cleansing of the public streets is well carried out, and as regards cleanliness, the streets of Hongkong will compare favourably with the streets of the cleanest towns in England.

The public markets are still in many ways in an indifferent condition, but the inspection of the food supplies in them is efficiently carried out. The system of their administration is in advance of food market administration in most English towns. In England, that powerful factor " vested interests " prevents the municipal authorities from doing that which they otherwise would do with regard to the management of their food markets. In a Colony of only 50 years standing, " vested interests " in matters of this kind do not count for much, although no opportunity is missed by those who have, or imagine they have such " vested interests," to prevent reforms for the public good being carried out.

FLORA.

The Flora of Hongkong comprises over 1,200 species, the importance of which to the botanist will be understood when it is considered that the late Mr. Bentham in his valuable work " Flora Hongkongensis " enumerated 1,056 species, which are distributed into 59 genera, and 125 natural orders. Since that time, discoveries new to botanical science have been, and are still being made; indeed, since 1861 to the present time, over 180 species have been added to Mr. Bentham's list. Scattered over the island may be found many trees, shrubs and plants, not only interesting to the ordinary observer, but valuable to the scientist. Hongkong is the natural home of the beautiful Rhodoleia Championi, as well as of several other well known plants, such as the Camellia, Azalea, long flowered lily, Strychinos, thorn apple, and Gelsemium. Ferns and orchids also abound on the island and are most varied and beautiful. There are woods at Little Hongkong and a few other localities where indigenous forest trees of Oak, Camphor, Hog Plum, Bread Fruit and many others, will be found.

FAUNA.

The Zoology of Hongkong is limited, as regards wild animals, to a small deer, a badger and a species of wild cat, but these are not numerous. The domestic animals, in addition to dogs and cats, are buffaloes, goats and pigs. Reptiles are numerous, and include pythons and snakes of various kinds (two of which only, the cobra and a green snake, popularly known as the bamboo snake, have been found to be poisonous); lizards, iguanas, bull and edible frogs, and newts. The insects are most numerous, comprising beetles of all kinds, mosquitoes, dragon flies, locusts, ants, wasps, bees, butterflies, moths, spiders, centipedes, scorpions, snails, worms, fire-flies, glow-worms, &c. White ants are also very common and destructive. Oysters, cuttlefish, sea stars, jelly fish and sea anemones are plentiful in the waters of the Colony. Since the first "Preservation of Bird's Ordinance" was passed in 1870, several kinds of birds now find their home undisturbed in the Colony. The Rapacious birds include sparrow hawks and kites. The Perching birds are goat suckers, king fishers, fly catchers, wagtails, tom tits, larks. house sparrows, Java sparrows, numerous magpies, of both large and small varieties. The climbing birds include several kinds of woodpeckers; and among the gallinaceous birds are peacock and other pheasants and numerous pigeons and doves. In the marshes and paddy fields adjoining some parts of the Canton River, rice birds, quail, teal, herons and snipe are found.

The following is a list of birds and reptiles caught in the Colony and presented to the City Hall Museum.

LIST OF HONGKONG BIRDS IN THE GIFT COLLECTION OF THE CITY HALL MUSEUM.

RAPTORES.

Falco æsalon.—Merlin.
Falco tinnunculus alaudarins.—Kestrel
Milvus melanotis.—Larger Indian kite.
Asio otus.—Long eared owl.

INSESSORES.

Steatornis caripensis.—Night-jar.
Sterna hirundo.—Sea swallow.
Alcedo atricapilla.—Black capped kingfisher.
Alcedo ispeda.—Common kingfisher.
Ceryle guttata.—Spotted kingfisher.
Halcyon smyrnensis.—White breasted kingfisher.
Lanius excubitor.—Great grey shrike or butcher bird.
Glareola Austriaca.—Austrian prating-cole.
Motacilla yarrellii.—Pied wagtail.
Troglodytes vulgaris.—Wren.
Garrulax Chinensis.—Black faced thrush.
Myophonus cæruleus.—Whistling thrush.
Pycnonotus atricapillus.—Black headed bulbul.
Urocissa sinensis.—Chinese treepie,
Pica caudata.—Magpie.
Acridotheres christatellus.—Mina.
Sturnus cineraceus.—Grey starling.

Amadina gouldiæ.—Gouldian finch.
Emberiza leucophry.—White crowned bunting.
Centropus rufipennis.—Crow pheasant.
Trochilus cyanurus.—Blue tailed humming bird.

RASORES.

Turtur auritus.—Turtle dove.
Columba viridis.—Green dove.
Francolinus perlatus.—Pearled partridge.

GRALLATORES.

Ardea egretta.—The white heron.
Ardea cinerea.—Common heron.
Ardeola Grayii.—Paddy bird.
Nycticorax griseus.—Night heron.
Platatea leucorodia.—Common spoon bill.
Gallinago gallinula.—Jack snipe.
Rallus virginianus.—Virginian rail.
Fulica atra. —Common coot.

NATATORES.

Cygnus atratus.—Black swan.
Mareca penelope.—Wigeon.
Mergus albellus.—Smew.
Larus canus.—Common gull.
Anas strepera.—Gadwall.
Podiceps minor.—Dabchick.
Diomedea exulans.—Wandering albatross.
Graculus carbo.—Cormorant.

LIST OF HONGKONG REPTILES
in the gift Collection of the City Hall Museum.

———

Bufo melanostictus.—The black spotted toad.
Bungarus fasciatus.
Bungarus semifasciatus.
Chrysopelea ornata.

Compoossoma radiatum.
Cyclophis major.
Dipsas multimaculata.
Eumeces quadrilinearis.—Lizard,
Gorduis.
Hemidactylus frœnatus.—Lizard,
Homalopsis buccata.
Hydrus major.—Sea snake.
Lycoodon aulicus.
Molge sinensis.
Naja tripudians.—The cobra da capello.
Ophiophagus elaps.
Pareas lævis.—Var.
Pelámys bicolor.—Marine snake.
Ptyas mucosus.
Python reticulatus.
Rana esculenta var.—The edible frog.
Rana figrina.—Six legged frog.
Rhacophorus maculatus.
Scolopendra concolor.
Simotes swinhonis.
Tachydromus meridionalis.
Trimeresurus erythrurus.
Trimeresurus gramineus,
Tropidonotus guincunciatus.
Tropidonotus stolatus.—Var.
Tropidonotus subminatus.
Typhlops braminus.

The City Hall Museum also contains a valuable and interesting collection of birds and reptiles as well as animals from India, China the Philippines and many other parts of the World.

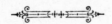

CHAPTER XII.

CANTON AND MACAO.

HONGKONG is so situated with regard to Canton and Macao, that most pleasant excursions may be made to them by the splendid service of river steamers, which leaves Hongkong daily, and no one who has two or three days to spare should miss the opportunity of a visit to these historic cities.

CANTON.

Canton is the capital of southern China, and is the most noted commercial city in the Chinese Empire, for its position, population, and wealth. It is only 90 miles distant from Hongkong, and is situated on the North bank of the Chu-kiang, or Pearl river, in latitude 23° 7′ North, and longtitude 113° 14′ East.

The name by which Canton is known to the Chinese is Kwang-chow-fu, or Stengcheng—the provincial capital;—the name Canton being derived from the old Portuguese manner of pronouncing Kwang-tung, the province immediately adjoining Hongkong of which Canton is the capital, and one of the eighteen provinces into which China proper is divided.

Canton owes its pre-eminence to its wonderful site at the junction of three remarkable rivers; the North, East, and West, which send their united waters into the sea through the Pearl river and other lesser channels connecting Canton with the China Sea. Canton was celebrated as one of the principal marts of commerce of the world a thousand years ago and yet owing to the conservative nature of the Chinese, all foreign commerce stops there and no foreigner can proceed further unless under special restrictions forbidding him to trade in the interior.

The City of Canton was surrounded by a wall eight centuries ago, but like the city of London it has long outgrown its limits and Canton without is now larger than Canton within the walls. The first Englishman to land at Canton was Captain Weddell who arrived there in command of a fleet of English merchant-men, so long ago as the year 1637, and he had to fight his way in through the Bogue forts. In 1684, the East India Company established themselves at Canton, and their Canton factory became celebrated throughout the world for its vastness and prosperity until the termination of their monopoly in 1834. The events linking Canton with Hongkong are summarised in the earlier chapters of this work.

Leaving Hongkong for Canton, the steamer threads its way through the western portion of the harbour and directs its course to the narrow channel known as the Cap shui mun separating the island of Lantao at its North-eastern extremity from the mainland, and then rounds westward into the broad estuary of the Canton river. Here the mountain scenery is most magnificent, the highest mountains of Lantao on the left, 4,000 feet high, being usually shrouded in mist. Castle Peak is seen on the right, and the steamer turning here due north, passes the historic island of Lintin to the left and in three hours after leaving Hongkong approaches Chuenpi and the Bogue forts. A little further on is Tiger Island (or as the Portuguese call it Bocca Tigris, the Tiger's mouth). This island rises about 400 feet above sea level and takes its name from its fanciful resemblance to a tiger's head. Passing Tiger Island, the steamer ascends the river through alluvial flats, highly cultivated with rice and sugar cane, and then arrives at the anchorage of Whampoa.

After leaving Whampoa, the steamer takes a channel between low banks, to the right. The chain of hills in the distance is known as the White Cloud range, and includes the White Cloud mountain behind Canton. On the opposite shore are two nine-storied pagodas, the first of which is called the Whampoa pagoda, and the second, nearer Canton, the First Bar pagoda. Soon after passing the Bar, the City of Canton with its walls and pagodas is in full view, the Roman Catholic Cathedral being conspicuous from its height and western architecture, so different from all other buildings of the City. Opposite to Canton is the island of Honam, famous for its temple. The river is crowded with trading junks and boats of every description. The foreign residences at Canton are erected on Shameen, (the sand flats), the site being leased to the English and French Governments in 1859. It is about 2850 feet in length by 950 at its greatest breadth and is separated from the Chinese suburb on its northern side, by a canal 100 feet wide. Shameen is inclosed from the river and canal by a massive embankment of granite which occupied two years in completion and upon which a sum of $325,000 was expended, the British Government paying four fifths, and the French one fifth. Shameen is pleasantly situated opposite a broad and deep channel of the river, known as the Macao passage, and is in immediate proximity to the western suburb, the centre of the Chinese wholesale trade, and near where all the principal merchants have their residences. The Shameen Hotel belonging to the Shameen Hotel Company Limited, a Hongkong Company, is the only hotel at Canton.

The sights at Canton are the temples, pagodas, city walls, on which are 12 gates, the water clock, the streets, the fa-ti gardens, the shops, and warehouses. Guides can be obtained on board the steamer or from the Shameen Hotel, and descriptive guide books to Canton can be obtained in Hongkong from Kelly and Walsh, Limited.

MACAO.

Macao is a Portuguese Colony and is situated upon a peninsula forming the southern extremity of Heung Shan island on the western side of the estuary of the Canton river, 40 miles West from Hongkong. The settlement dates back to the year 1557. It was at first governed by the senior captains of the Portuguese trading vessels in China, but in less than 30 years the population had increased to nearly 20,000 in number, when it was given the name of Cidade do Santo Nome de Deos en China, or the city of the Holy Name of God, and is to this day frequently spoken of as the Holy City. Macao continued to flourish as a trading centre, particularly during the period when trade with China was developed by the East India Company who kept a large establishment there, but when the British community were forced to leave Macao during the first Chinese war, and Hongkong was ceded in 1841 as a British Colony, Macao began to decline altogether.

One of the magnificent river steamers of the Hongkong, Canton and Macao Steamboat Company, Limited, leaves Hongkong for Macao daily at 2 p.m. and threading its way westward through the harbour, turns southward through the Sulphur channel between Hongkong and Green Island ; then steering westward again to the channel between Lantao and the small island of Chang Chow, passes along the southern side of Lantao. On the western side of Chang Chow, which is one of the throat gates of Hongkong, is a large Chinese Village and a Chinese Customs Station. The cruise along the coast of Lantao and between that and the many islands lying off the coast is extremely interesting and pleasant.

From the western end of Lantao to Macao is the broad estuary of the Canton river, and in three and a half or four hours after leaving Hongkong, according to the state of the tide, the steamer passes in front of Macao and turning round the peninsula passes the Fort of St. Thiago da Barra, or Bar Fort into the inner harbour of Macao, to its wharf there.

Macao is built upon the declivities of a hill rising from two hundred to three hundred feet above sea level. North of this about three miles from the extreme end of the peninsula, the hill slopes away to a narrow neck of sand where is the stone barrier and small military station dividing the settlement of Macao from the rest of the island of Heung shan, which is Chinese territory.

There are two good hotels at Macao, the Boa Vista erected on a hill near the southern extremity of the city, and Hing Kee's hotel on the Praya Grande surrounded by trees and facing South East.

The objects of interest at Macao are the Cathedral and four parish Churches, none of which are distinguished by special architectural features. The most picturesque object in the buildings of Macao is the stone facade of the collegiate church of St. Paul erected in the sixteenth century. The building, all but the facade was destroyed by fire in 1835. Of the twenty pillars left standing, the ten lower are of the Ionic and the upper ten of the Corinthian order. In the niches are statues, one representing the Mother of God, and the others St. Paul and other Saints.

The Praya Grande extending along the bay in front of the town forms an excellent promenade or Marine Parade of a little more than half a mile in length. In the centre of the bay is Government House. On Penha Hill at the South-west end, is the small fort of Bom Parto and above it the Boa Vista Hotel. At the East end of the Praya Grande are the Public Gardens, Military Barracks and Fort St. Francisco.

The most prominent fort of Macao is Fort Guia, crowning the lofty hill of that name upon which also stands the lighthouse, sending forth after sunset a revolving light over the Macao roads. The largest fort is that of St. Paulo do Monte, commouly known as the Monte fort. It was built on the summit of the Monte or Hill of St. Paul in 1626 and commands the whole of the City with its 48 guns. There are also many other smaller forts guarding Macao from the outer world, but they are not of a dangerous description, and a shell from a gun of modern calibre would be sufficient to destroy each one of them.

A favourite walk or ride by jinricksha—the jinrickshas are very good, and their price very moderate at Macao—is to the Point at the end of the road running through the central portion of the peninsula, either by that road, or by the sea road, which commences at the east end of the Praya Grande, and is carried round the cliffs, passes under the lighthouse, and by Casilhas Bay, and the Point to the Barrier, where the Chinese road commences.

Near the Point is the Protestant Cemetery and the Tennis Courts.

The British Chapel is situated in the North-western portion of Macao adjoining the entrance to Camoens' Gardens. It is a small building containing about 40 sittings. Adjoining the chapel is the old Protestant Cemetery, where are a large number of monuments to English and Americans, who have died in the Far East. Among these will be found the tombs of Admiral Sir Philip le Fleming Senhouse who died at Hongkong on the 13th June, 1841, while commanding Her Majesty's squadron in China and of the Right Hon. Lord Henry Churchill, Captain of the *Druid* and fifth son of the late Duke of Marlborough. There are also monuments to the Rev. Robert Morrison the celebrated sinalogue, and to his son the late Mr. J. R. Morrison, a distinguished interpreter in the early days of Hongkong.

Camoens' Gardens is the one celebrated place to which every visitor to Macao must go, or he has not been to Macao at all. The entrance adjoins the British chapel, and passing through a small flower garden, the path leads into a shrubbery in which are also forest trees of banyan, jack fruit and others, furnishing a thick shade. Pathways lead through the shrubbery and to Camoens' Grotto. This is a huge granite boulder, with a cleft caused by weathering. Another huge boulder superposed forms an archway to the cleft. In this retreat Camoens is supposed to have composed his Lusiad, in which he sang the glories and conquests of his country. Here a bust of Camoens has been placed upon a pedestal, upon which have been cut some verses from the Lusiad.

Luis Camoens is deemed the most celebrated poet of Portugal. He was born at Lisbon in 1527. He entered the army and served with great repute in Africa against the Moors. On his return to Portugal in 1553, he engaged in an expedition to the East Indies, but incurring the displeasure of the authorities by a satire upon the Viceroy of Goa and others of his countrymen, he was sent in 1556 to Macao where he held a small official post.

He eventually returned to Lisbon, and although shipwrecked on his passage home, he succeeded in preserving the manuscript of his poem, which was published in 1569. His death occurred ten years later in a charitable institute.

The small island in the Inner Harbour at the North-western end of Macao is called Green Island. Upon this island have been erected the extensive buildings, machinery and kilns of the Green Island Cement Company, Limited, a Hongkong Company, which are well worth a visit. The stone is brought down in boats from the limestone mountains in the interior, beyond Canton, and the other materials are at hand in the mud of the Inner Harbour. Green Island is under the control of the Bishop of Macao, who has a residence erected on the island.

Macao is famous for its gambling houses in which Fantan has its principal home. No gambling is allowed in Hongkong but the great games of chance of China are permitted at Macao and Kowloon City. One of the most important heads of revenue of Macao as of Kowloon City, is the income produced from the licencing of the gambling houses, the bulk of which, it is almost needless to say is derived from Hongkong, the centre of the gambling spirits of South China.

An interesting excursion from Macao is that to the hot springs of Yung Mak on the island of Heung Shan, about twenty miles North-north-west from Macao. The temperature of the water coming from these springs is about 170°. They are situated in a valley surrounded by high mountains and from the position of the springs at the centre of the circle of mountains, it is generally considered that the site is that of an extinct volcano. The springs occupy a space of some seventy or eighty square yards and steam arises from the whole of this space. The springs are shallow and vary their number and position from time to time, but there are generally three of from eight to ten feet in diameter. The water is clear and salt without bitterness. A paddle-boat leaves Macao for Yung Mak at 8 o'clock every morning, returning from the village about 3 in the afternoon.

A frequent excursion from Macao is to the Valley of the Ringing Rocks on Lappa island across the inner harbour. A pathway winds through the hills and follows the course of a streamlet for about a mile until a ravine is reached, in which is a torrent of granite boulders piled one above the other in great tumult. Two of these boulders when struck send forth a clear ringing sound like a church bell, which circumstance has given the name to the valley.

Steamers leave every other day from Macao to Canton, or the return journey from Macao to Hongkong may be most comfortably accomplished by the river steamers of the Hongkong Canton and Macao Steamboat Company leaving Macao at 8 a.m. As the steamer emerges from the Inner Harbour and passes in front of the Praya Grande into the open estuary of the Canton river with the eastern Sun throwing its glamour over the churches, forts and buildings of the City, the opening words of Sir John Bowring's ode to Macao will form a fitting farewell—

> Gem of the orient earth and open sea,
> Macao! that in thy lap and on thy breast
> Hast gathered beauties all the loveliest.

The End.

Printed by Kelly & Walsh, Ld., Hongkong.

Legalised Tariff of Fares for Chairs,
Jinrickshas, and Sampans.

——— ✑ ———

Chairs.

PLACE.	½ Hour.	1 Hour.	3 Hours.	6 Hours.	Day 6 a.m. to 6 p.m.
1.—* In VICTORIA, with two bearers ...	0.10	0.20	0.50	0.70	1.00
2.—Beyond VICTORIA, with four bearers ...	—	0.60	1.00	1.50	2.00
3.—In the HILL DISTRICTS, with two bearers	0.15	0.30	0.75	1.00	1.50
4.—In the HILL DISTRICTS, with four bearers	—	0.60	1.00	1.50	2.00

* If the trip is extended beyond VICTORIA, half fare extra.

———

Jinrickshas.

(With single drawer).

Quarter hour	...	...	...	...	...	5 *cents.*
Half hour ...	...	...	...	...	...	10 ,,
Hour	...	...	...	...	...	15 ,,
Every subsequent hour	...	...	...	...	10 ,,

NOTE.—Victoria extends from Mount Davis to Causeway Bay and up to the level of Robinson Road. If the vehicle is discharged beyond these limits half fare extra is to be allowed for the return journey. Extra bearers or drivers and extra hours to be paid proportionate sums.

———

Rowing Boat or Sampans.

Hour with 2 passengers ... ... 20 *cents.*
Half hour with 2 passengers ... ... 10 ,,

For each extra passenger 5 cents for half-an-hour, 10 cents per hour. Between sunset and sunrise 5 cents extra per passenger.

ADVERTISEMENTS.

KELLY & WALSH, Ld.

19, Queen's Road, Central, HONGKONG.

AND AT

SHANGHAI, YOKOHAMA and SINGAPORE.

SELECTED ✦ LIST ✦ OF ✦ BOOKS

RELATING TO THE

FAR EAST.

A Hand-Book for Travellers in Japan (Murray's Guide).—
Third Edition, revised and for the most part re-written by BASIL
HALL CHAMBERLAIN, Professor of Japanese and Philology in
the Imperial University of Japan, and W. B. MASON, late of
the Imperial Japanese Department of Communications, with
15 Maps. Crown 8vo. Cloth $4.50

The Real Japan.—
Studies of Contemporary Japanese Manners, Morals, Adminis-
tration and Politics, by HENRY NORMAN, illustrated from
Photographs by the Author. Demy 8vo. Cloth $3.00
    Ditto   Cheap Edition $1.50

Jinrikisha Days in Japan.—
By ELIZA RUHAMAH SCIDMORE, illustrated. Crown 8vo.
Cloth $3.00

Things Japanese.—
Being Notes on various subjects connected with Japan. By
BASIL HALL CHAMBERLAIN, Professor of Japanese and
Philology in the Imperial University of Japan. Demy 8vo.
Cloth $3.00

A Social Departure.—
How Orthodocia and I went round the World by Ourselves. By
SARA JEANETTE DUNCAN, with 111 illustrations by F. H.
Townsend. New Edition. Crown 8vo. Cloth $3.00

Japanese Jingles.—
Being a few little verses that have appeared before in the "Japan
Gazette." By MAE ST. JOHN BRAMHALL, beautifully printed
in colour in Japanese style on Japanese crêpe paper $0.50

A Trip Round the World.—

In 1887-8. By W. S. CAINE. M.P., illustrations by John Pedder, H.
SHEPPERD DALE and the Author. Demy 8vo. Cloth   .. $1.50

The Soul of the Far East.—

By PERCIVAL LOWELL. Foolscap 8vo. Cloth $2.00

The Light of Asia or the Great Renunciation.—

Being the Life and Teaching of Gautama, Prince of India and
Founder of Buddhism, as told in verse by an Indian Buddhist.
By Sir Edwin Arnold, M.A., K.C.I.E. Foolscap 8vo. Cloth $1.50

Tales of Old Japan.—

By A. B. MITFORD, with wood-cuts. Demy 8vo. $1.00

Seas and Lands.—

Reprinted from the "Daily Telegraph" from Letters addressed to
that Journal by Sir Edwin Arnold, K.C.I.E., with illustrations.
Crown 8vo. $1.00

The Pictorial Arts of Japan.—

With a brief Historical Sketch of the Associated Arts and some
remarks upon the Pictorial Art of the Chinese and Coreans,
by WM. ANDERSON, F.R.G.S., late Medical Officer to H. M.
Legation in Japan, superbly illustrated. Folio. ½ Morocco .. $60.00

Le Japon Artistique.—

Documents d'Art. et d'Industrie, rèunis par S. BING. 3 Vols.
Imperial 4to. $25.00

Handy Guide to the Japanese Islands.—

By H. W. SETON KEER, F.R.G.S., with Map and Plans $1.00

Keeling's Guide to Japan.—

Yokohama, Tokio, Hakone, Fujiama, Kamakura, Yokoska,
Kanozan, Narita, Nikko, Kioto, Osaka, Kobe, &c., &c.,
together with useful Hints, History, Customs, Festivals,
Roads, &c., &c. with ten Maps. Fourth Edition revised and
enlarged by A. FARSARI (second issue)..   ..   ..   .. $1.00

The Official Railway & Steamboat Travellers' Guide.—

With General information for Tourists in Japan $3.00

The Mikado's Empire.—

History of Japan and personal experience, observations and
Studies in Japan, 1870-1874, by W. E. GRIFFIS with supple-
ment, Japan in 1883 and 1886   ..   .. $6.50

Verdant Simple's Views of Japan. —

Or 'The Contents of his Note Book.' By GRENON $0.50

A Pocket Book of Japanese Words and Phrases.—

By A. FARSARI $0.75

Japan, Travels and Researches.—
Undertaken at the cost of the Prussian Government. By J. J.
REIN, with 20 Illustrations and 2 Maps .. 　.. 　.. 　.. $9.00

The Industries of Japan.—
Together with an account of its Agriculture, Forestry, Arts and
Commerce. By J. J. REIN, with 44 Illustrations and 3 Maps $12.00

Japanese Pottery.—
With notes describing the thoughts and subjects employed in its
decoration, with Illustrations. By JAMES L. BOWES .. 　.. $24.00

Japan and its Art.—
By MARCUS B. HUISH, profusely Illustrated 　.. 　.. 　.. $5.00

Rand McNally's Map of Japan.—
In two Sections .. 　.. 　.. 　.. 　.. 　.. 　.. 　.. $1.00

Handbook of Colloquial Japanese.—
By BASIL HALL CHAMBERLAIN 　.. 　.. 　.. 　.. $3.50

English and Japanese Conversations.—
By T. INOUYE .. 　.. 　.. 　.. 　.. 　.. 　.. 　.. $1.00

Noto.—
An unexplored corner of Japan. By PERCIVAL LOWELL 　.. $2.00

A Dictionary of the Principal Roads.—
Chief Towns and Villages of Japan. By W. N. WHITNEY, M.D. $1.50

A Japanese-English and English-Japanese Dictionary.—
By J. C. HEPBURN 　.. 　.. 　.. 　.. 　.. 　.. $2.00
Ditto 　　Large Edition 　.. 　.. 　.. 　.. 　.. $7.50

Handbook of English Japanese Etymology.—
By W. IMBRIE .. 　.. 　.. 　.. 　.. 　.. 　.. 　.. $2.00

Japanese Pottery.—
By A. W. FRANKS 　.. 　.. 　.. 　.. 　.. 　.. 　.. $2.00

The Chrysanthemum.—
A monthly Magazine of Japan, 1881 .. 　.. 　.. 　.. 　.. $3.50

Oyuchusan.—
A Japanese Song set to Music and quaintly illustrated by native
artists. By Lieut. BOSTWICK, U.S.N. 　.. 　.. 　.. 　.. $0.60

Orient and Occident.—
A journey Eastward from Lahore to Liverpool *via* the Canadian
Pacific Railway 　.. 　.. 　.. 　.. 　.. 　.. 　.. $3.50

The Great Earthquake of Japan 1891.—
A Magnificent Album of Photographs by Professor Burton, with
descriptive Letterpress by Professor Milne. Imperial ob. 4to. $10.00

Japonica.—
By Sir EDWIN ARNOLD, K.C.I.E. with illustrations by Robert
Blum. Imperial 8vo. Cloth. Printed on plate paper 　.. $5.00

The Multum in Parvo Atlas of the World.—
    Containing 96 Maps $1.00

The Philippine Islands.—
    A Historical, Geographical, Ethnographical, Social and Commer-
    cial Sketch of the Philippine Archipelago and its Political
    Dependencies. By JOHN FOREMAN, F.R.G.S. In 1 Vol.
    Demy 8vo. 500 pages, with Map and Frontispiece. Cloth
    extra $5.00
        "Comprehensive in its range and picturesque in its details, enlivened
    by abundance of personal anecdote, and equipped with much statistical
    information."—*Times.*
        "Abounds in traits, anecdotes and acute observations."—*Athenæum.*

Rambles through Japan without a Guide.—
    By ALBERT TRACY $2.50

The Garden of Japan.—
    A Year's Diary of its Flowers by F. S. PIGGOTT, with four
    Pictures by Alfred East, R.I.   ..   .. $6·50

The Japs at Home.—
    By DOUGLAS SLADEN $6.00

JAPANESE CHILDREN'S BOOKS.

Japanese Fairy Tales.—
    A series of stories translated from the Japanese. Printed on
    Japanese crêpe paper and illustrated in colours by Native
    Artists   ..   .. 25 cents each

BOOKS ON CHINA.

Things Chinese.—
    Being Notes on Various Subjects connected with China. By J.
    DYER BALL, M.R.A.S.   Second Edition, revised and greatly
    enlarged. Demy 8vo. Cloth $3.50

New China and Old.—
    Personal Recollections and Observations of Thirty Years. By
    the Ven. ARTHUR E. MOULE, B.D., Archdeacon in Mid-China.
    Illustrated $3.00

Pidgin-English Sing Song.—
    Or Songs and Stories in the China-English Dialect, with a
    Vocabulary. By CHARLES G. LELAND $1.50

Lays of Far Cathay and others.—
    A Collection of original Poems. By "TUNG CHIA." Illustrated $2.00

The Truth About Opium.—
  By W. BRERETON $2.50

Flora Hongkongensis.—
  A Description of the Flowering Plants and Ferns of the Island of
    Hongkong. By GEO. BENTHAM, with Map $9.00

Guide to Kuan Hua.—
  Translation of the Chinese Work "Kuang Hua Chih Nan." By
    L. C. HOPKINS $2.00

Among the Mongols.—
  By REV. JAS. GILMOUR $2.50

The Authentic Map of China and Japan.—
  Mounted on Linen folded in neat Cloth Covers $1.00

Stanford's Map of China and Japan.—
  Mounted in Case $4.00

Corea, or the Hermit Nation.
  By W. E. GRIFFIS $5.00

Child Life in China.—
  By Mrs. BRYSON $2.00

China Coast Tales.—
  By "LISE BOEHM." $1.00

Leng-Tso, the Chinese Bible Woman.—
  By REV. J. A. DAVIS $2.00

Among the Sons of Han.—
  Notes of a Six Years' Residence in various parts of China and
    Formosa, with Map. By Mrs. T. F. HUGHES $3.50

Chinese Commercial Guide.—
  Containing Treaties, Tariff and Tables useful in the Trade of
    China and Eastern Asia. By S. WELLS WILLIAMS $6.00

La Province Chinoise du Yun Nan.—
  By EMILE ROCHER. 2 Vols. $2.50

The Manchus.—
  Or the Reigning Dynasty of China, their Rise and Progress,
    with Maps and Illustrations. By REV. JOHN ROSS $5.00

From Kulja, across the Tian Shan to Lob-Nor.—
  By Colonel PREJEVALSKY $7.50

Journey of Augustus R. Margary.—
  From Shanghae to Bhamo and back to Manwyne, with Preface.
    By Sir RUTHERFORD ALCOCK, K.C.B. $3.50

Through the Yangtse Gorges.—
  Or Trade and Travel in Western China. By ARCHIBALD JOHN
    LITTLE, F.R.G.S. $4.00

The Divine Classic of Nan Hua.—

    Being the works of Chuang Tse, translated by FRED.
      HENRY BALFOUR, F.R.G.S...   ..   .. $4.00

How we got to Pekin.—

    A narrative of the Campaign in China of 1860. By Rev. R. J. L.
      MCGHEE $2.50

The Straits of Malacca, Indo-China and China.

    By J. THOMSON $4.00

Wanderings in China.—

    By C. T. GORDON CUMMING $4.00

Treaty Ports of China and Japan.—

    A complete Guide to the open Ports of those countries. By
      MAYERS AND DENNYS 1867   ..   .. $10.00

Chuang Tzu, Mystic, Moralist and Social Reformer.—

    Translated from the Chinese. By H. A. GILES $3.50

Chinese Music.—

    With Illustrations. By J. A. VAN AALST $2.00

Three Lectures on Buddhism.—

    By ERNEST J. EITEL, PH.D. $1.50

Hung Lou Meng.—

    Or the Dream of the Red Chamber. A Chinese Novel translated
      by H. BENCRAFT JOLY $3.50

Mongolia and the Solitudes of Northern Thibet.—

    By Colonel PREJEVALSKY. 2 Vols. $18.00

Erh Tou Mei.—

    Ou Les Pruniers Merveilleux ; traduit par A. T. PIRY. 2 Vols. $4.00

Home Life in China.—

    By Mrs. M. L. BRYSON..   ..   .. $2.00

Ordre Du Double Dragon.— $2.50

Across Chrysé.—

    Being the narrative of a journey of exploration through the
    South China Border lands from Canton to Mandalay. By
    ARCHIBALD R. COLQUHOUN. 2 Vols. $6.50

Among the Shans.—

    By ARCHIBALD R. COLQUHOUN, with 50 Illustrations, &c.   .. $5.00

China.—

    A descriptive account of the country and the manners and
    customs of the people. By Prof. ROBERT K. DOUGLAS, with
    Map and numerous illustrations $2.00

The Dragon, Image and Demon.—
> Or the three religions of China—Confucianism, Buddhism and Taoism, giving an account of the Mythology, Idolatry and Demonolatry of the Chinese. By Rev. HAMPDEN C. DUBOSE $3.50

Typical Women of China.—
> Abridged from the Chinese work : "Records of Virtuous Women of Ancient and Modern Times." By Miss A. C. SAFFORD. Imp. 16mo, Cloth, with numerous illustrations $1.00

Chinese Stories.—
> By ROBERT K. DOUGAS ; with illustrations $5.50

The Religions Systems of China.—
> Its ancient Forms, Evolution. History and Present Aspect, Manners, Customs and Social Institutions connected therewith by J. J. M. DEGROOT, PH.D. Book I. Disposal of the Dead .. $6.00

BOOKS FOR THE STUDY OF CHINESE.

Cantonese Made Easy.—
> By J. DYER BALL, M.R.A.S. Second Edition, Revised and Enlarged $3.00

The Cantonese-Made-Easy Vocabulary.—
> By J. DYER BALL, M.R.A.S. $1.00

An English-Cantonese Pocket Vocabulary.—
> Without the Chinese Characters or Tonic Marks, &c. By J. DYER BALL, M.R.A.S. $0.75

Easy Sentences in the Hakka Dialect.—
> With a Vocabulary. By J. DYER BALL, M.R.A.S. $1.00

How to Write the Radicals.—
> By J. DYER BALL, M.R.A.S. $0.75

How to Speak Cantonese.—
> Fifty conversations in Cantonese Colloquial. By J. DYER BALL, M.R.A.S. $3.00

How to Write Chinese.—
> By J. DYER BALL, M.R.A.S. $2.00

Select Phrases in the Canton Dialect.—
> By Dr. KERR. Third Edition, Revised and Classified $0.50

Notes on the Chinese Documentary Style.
> By F. HIRTH, PH.D. $1.50

Text Book of Documentary Chinese.—
> With a Vocabulary. Edited by F. HIRTH, PH.D. 2 Vols. .. $4.00

Wen Chien Tzu Erh Chi.—
A Series of Papers selected as specimens of Documentary Chinese designed to assist Students of the Language, as written by the Officials of China. 2 Vols. $4.50

Tzu Erh Chi.—
Colloquial Series. By Sir THOMAS WADE, F.R.G.S.   3 Vols   .. $15.00

English and Cantonese Dictionary.—
By JOHN CHALMERS, LL.D. Sixth Edition $3.00

Essays on the Chinese Language.—
By T. WATTERS..   ..   .. $3.50

Elementary Lessons in Chinese.—
By Rev. ARNOLD FOSTER $1.00

Chinese without a Teacher.—
Being a collection of easy and useful sentences in the Mandarin Dialect with a Vocabulary. By HERBERT A. GILES $1.00

Progressive and Idiomatic Sentences in Cantonese Colloquial.—
By Rev. A. A. FULTON $1.00

Æsops Fable's in English and Chinese —
Part 1. Translated by A. J. MAY $0.50

A Manual of Chinese Quotations.—
Being a translation of the *Shing ü Háu* with text, notes, explanations, and an index for easy reference. By J. H. STEWART LOCKHART, F.R.G.S., M.R.A.S., &c., Registrar General, Hongkong $5.00

A Chinese-English Dictionary.—
By HERBERT A. GILES, H.B.M. Consul at Ningpo. Price, complete in 3 parts $35.00

BOOKS ON HONGKONG.

Kelly & Walsh's Hand Book to Hongkong $1.00

Our Island.—
A Naturalist's description of Hongkong by Sydney B. J. SKERTCHLY F.G.S., M.A.I. (late of H. M. GEOLOGICAL SURVEY) $1.00

Kelly & Walsh's Album of Honghong.—
Containg 19 Views of the Colony, reproduced from Photographs by Griffith $1.00

KELLY & WALSH, Ld.

CHEAP AND LIGHT LITERATURE.—

We receive nearly all the NEWEST BOOKS by the FOREMOST WRITERS OF THE DAY in a CHEAP FORM, *Published exclusively for circulation in the Colonies,* simultaneously with their issue as expensive first editions in Great Britain.

We have also on hand in cheap paper covers, most of the Standard Works of Fiction by the best English Authors.

PHOTOGRAPHS.—

Tourists should not fail to inspect our splended collection of PHOTOGRAPHS OF HONGKONG AND CANTON. We sell them at the same prices as at the Studio.

TOBACCOS, CIGARETTES AND CIGARS.—

We are the largest Importers of Tobaccos and Cigarettes in the Colony. and have on hand a greater variety of Brands than can be found elsewhere. Purchasers may depend upon our Goods being absolutely fresh; our system being to buy in small quantities and at frequent intervals. The following is a selection of our leading Brands.

TOBACCOS.—

Capstan Navy Cut—Ogden's Fruit and Honey—Ogden's Navy Cut—Ogden's Silver Veil—Ogden's Best Bird's Eye—Wills' Bristol Bird's Eye—Wills' Three Castles—Wills' Golden Flake Honey Dew—Wills' Traveller Brand—Happy Thought—Dollar Brand—Star Mixture—Golden Eagle—Cope's Golden Cloud—Cope's Bird's Eye—Cope's Navy Cut—Pioneer Brand—St. Ledger Flake Cut—Smoking Mixture—Moose Head Scroll Cut.

CIGARETTES.—

Three Castles—Wills' Firefly—Ogden's Bird's Eye—Sweet Caporals—Kinney's Straight Cuts—Golden Pheasant—Bright Virginia—Sweet Briar—Daisy.

MANILA CIGARS.—

Londres—Regalia Britannica—Regalia Imperial—Orien talss—Exquisitos—Regalia Filipina—Regalia Antonia Lopez—Princessas—Media Regalia—Brevas—Carolinas—Regalia Comme il faut.

HONGKONG—SHANGHAI—YOKOHAMA—SINGAPORE.

Mactavish & Lehmann, Ld.,

DISPENSING CHEMISTS AND WHOLESALE DRUGGISTS,

PERFUMERS,

Dealers in all kinds of Photographic Apparatus and Chemicals,

AND

AËRATED WATER MANUFACTURERS,

Outport Orders and Medical Missionaries have their orders attended to with great punctuality.

Head Office & Laboratory:—No. 1, The Bund, Shanghai.

Branches:—The Hongkew Medical Hall, Hongkew.
Tientsin Dispensary, Tientsin.
Hankow Dispensary, Hankow.

L'Hotel des Colonies,

LIMITED.

72   RUE MONTAUBAN   72

THIS HOTEL HAS BEEN ENTIRELY RENOVATED AND AFFORDS FIRST CLASS ACCOMMODATION TO VISITORS.

——:o:——

FAMILY HOTEL

WHICH IS COMPLETELY SEPARATED FROM THE PUBLIC BUILDING.

TERMS MODERATE.

NORTHERN PACIFIC STEAMSHIP CO.

AND

NORTHERN PACIFIC RAILROAD CO.

THE SHORT ROUTE BETWEEN
CHINA, JAPAN, THE UNITED STATES
CANADA AND EUROPE
viâ
THE INLAND SEA OF JAPAN AND THE YELLOWSTONE
NATIONAL PARK.

REGULAR Sailings between Hongkong and Tacoma calling at Shanghai, Kobe, Yokohama, and Victoria, B.C.

The Steamers of this line have most comfortable passenger accommodation, the cabins being large, airy, and well ventilated. Not more than two passengers are located in one State Room. The Cuisine is of the best and the steamers carry a duly qualified Surgeon as well as a Stewardess.

Among the attractions of this line may be mentioned the magnificent Scenery of the Inland Sea of Japan, of Puget sound, and of the Rocky Mountains, while the wonders of the Yellowstone Park need no mention.

From Tacoma to Chicago two trains run daily without any change of sleeping, dining, or drawing room cars. These trains are composed of the finest cars yet built, and the run from Tacoma to Chicago is made in 78 hours. From Chicago to New York passengers have the choice of the many well known routes, and this portion of the journey can be accomplished in 24 hours.

Passengers for Europe may cross the Atlantic by any Line of Steamers.

The Journey may be broken in Japan, and at any points of interest on the Railroad, provided timely notice is given to the Agents.

For time tables, rates of passage, and further information apply to any office of the NORTHERN PACIFIC RAILROAD or to—

DODWELL CARLILL & Co.
General Agents.

HONGKONG,
FOOCHOW, SHANGHAI, KOBE, YOKOHAMA,
VICTORIA, B.C., OR TACOMA.

HONGKONG, May, 1893.

THE
HONGKONG HIGH-LEVEL TRAMWAYS
COMPANY, LIMITED.

———>●<———

PEAK TRAMWAY.

———

No Traveller shouid miss a trip to the Peak. The most beautiful views, which compare favourably with any in the World, can be obtained within easy distance of the PEAK TERMINUS. The time occupied in the ascent is Nine Minutes and Cars run at the following times:—

———

TIME TABLE.

—

WEEK DAYS.

7.30 a.m. to 10.30 a.m.	- - -	Every quarter of an hour.
11.30 a.m. to 12.30 p.m.	- - -	Every half hour.
12.30 p.m. to 2.30 p.m.	- - -	Every quarter of an honr.
3.30 p.m. to 8.00 p.m.	- - -	Every quarter of an hour.

Night cars at 8.45 p.m. and 9 p.m. and from 9.45 p.m.
to 11.15 p.m. every half hour.

———

SATURDAYS.

Extra Cars at 11.30 p.m. and 11.45 p.m.

———

SUNDAYS.

10.30 a.m. and 10 40 a.m.

Noon to 2 p.m.	- - -	Every quarter of an hour.
3 p.m. to 8 p.m.	- - -	Every quarter of an hour.
Night cars from 9 p.m. to 11 p.m.		Every half hour.

JOHN D. HUMPHREYS & SON,
General Managers.

| THE EASTERN EXTENSION AUSTRALASIA & CHINA TELEGRAPH COMPANY, LIMITED. | THE GREAT NORTHERN TELEGRAPH COMPANY OF COPENHAGEN. |

RATE PER WORD
CHARGED AT THE COMPANIES' STATIONS.
IN
CHINA.

	HONGKONG.		FOOCHOW and AMOY.		SHANGHAI.		MACAO.	
	Via Eastern.	*Via* Northern.	*Via* Eastern.	*Via* Northern.	*Via* Eastern.	*Via* Northern.	*Via* Eastern.	*Via* Northern.
	\$ c.	\$ c.	\$ c.	\$ c.	\$ c.	\$ c.	\$ c.	\$ c.
EUROPE :—								
GREAT BRITAIN and all other Countries except.	2.30	2.30	2.30	2.30	2.30	2.30	2.45	2.45
RUSSIA in EUROPE and CAUCASUS.	2.30	1.75	2.30	1.75	2.30	1.75	2.45	1.85
ASIA :—								
CHINA :—								
Hongkong	...	...	0.33	0.33	0.44	0.44	0.12	0.12
Shanghai	0.44	0.44	0.33	0.33	...	...	0.56	0.56
Amoy	0.33	0.33	0.33	0.33	0.33	0.33	0.45	0.45
Foochow	0.33	0.33	0.33	0.33	0.33	0.33	0.45	0.45
Canton	...	...	0.43	0.43	0.54	0.54	0.22	...
COCHIN CHINA	0.60	2.95	0.93	2.95	1.04	2.95	0.75	3.05
JAVA	1.35	3.20	1.68	3.20	1.79	3.20	1.50	3.30
JAPAN :—								
Nagasaki	1.26	1.26	1.12	1.12	...	0.70	1.40	1.40
Other places	1.40	1.40	1.26	1.26	...	0.84	1.54	1.54
INDIA	1.80	2.50	2.13	2.50	2.24	2.50	1.90	2.60
Burmah	1.90	2.55	2.23	2.55	2.34	2.55	1.98	2.65
Ceylon	1.85	2.55	2.18	2.55	2.29	2.55	1.95	2.65
MANILA	0.70	...	1.03	1.03	1.14	1.14	0.80	...
PENANG	1.35	2.90	1.68	2.90	1.79	2.90	1.45	3.00
SINGAPORE	1.05	3.10	1.38	3.10	1.49	3.10	1.15	3.25
SIAM (via Saigon)	0.80	3.05	1.13	3.05	1.24	3.05	0.90	3.15
TONKIN (direct)	0.40	...	0.75	...	0.84	...	0.50	...
AUSTRALASIA :—								
NEW SOUTH WALES	2.20	2.90	2.53	2.90	2.64	2.90	2.30	3.00
NEW ZEALAND	2.30	2.95	2.63	2.95	2.74	2.95	2.40	3.05
QUEENSLAND	3.00	4.50	3.33	4.50	3.44	4.50	3.10	4.60
SOUTH AUSTRALIA	2.15	2.85	2.48	2.85	2.59	2.85	2.25	2.95
TASMANIA	2.40	3.00	2.73	3.00	2.84	3.00	2.50	3.15
VICTORIA	2.20	2.85	2.53	2.85	2.64	2.85	2.30	3.00
WESTERN AUSTRALIA	2.15	2.85	2.48	2.85	2.59	2.85	2.25	2.95

Complete Lists of Rates to all parts of the World can be obtained on application at the Companies' Offices.

THE
HONGKONG HOTEL.

OVERLOOKING THE HARBOUR.

(Facing Pedder Wharf, the principal Landing Stage of the Colony).

HAVING recently undergone very extensive alterations and additions, is now the Most Commodious and best Appointed Hotel in the East, and the only FIRST CLASS HOTEL in the City, affording Unequalled Accommodation to Travellers and others. It is situated in the Centre of the Town, opposite the General Post Office and the Hongkong Club, and in close proximity to the Banks and Shipping Office.

The MAIN ENTRANCE is in Pedder Street, and other Entrances lead from Queen's Road and Praya Central.

The Hotel STEAM LAUNCH conveys Passengers and Baggage to and from all Mail Steamers.

The TABLE D'HOTE, at Separate Tables, is supplied with Every Delicacy obtainable in the East, and the Cuisine in under Experienced Supervision.

The WINES and SPIRITS are selected by an expert, and the best Brands only are supplied.

The BED-ROOMS, with adjoining Bath Rooms, are Lofty and Well Ventilated, open on to Spacious Verandahs, and are fitted throughout with Electric Communicators.

The READING, WRITING, and SMOKING ROOMS (overlooking the Harbour), Ladies' DRAWING-ROOM, the Splendid New BAR and PUBLIC BILLIARD ROOMS (Six English and American Tables), are fitted with Every Convenience.

A handsomely appointed GRILL ROOM, where Chops, Steaks, &c., are served at any hour, adjoins the Hotel and is under the same management.

HYDRAULIC ASCENDING ROOMS of the latest and most approved type convey Passengers and Baggage from the Entrance Hall to each of the five floor above.

NIGHT PORTERS and WATCHMEN are continually on duty.

PERFECT SANITATION throughout the building has been made a special feature in the reconstruction of the late additions to the Hotel.

R. TUCKER,
Manger.

"VICTORIA" AND "PEAK" HOTELS.
HONGKONG.

These **commodious** and **well appointed** Hotels, being now under one management, are enabled to offer to Visitors and Residents, advantages and conveniences unpossessed by any other establishment in Hongkong.

The **VICTORIA HOTEL** is situated in the **most central** part of the City, and has **very superior accommodation** for Travellers, Boarders and Families.

The **PEAK HOTEL** is situated at Victoria Gap, at a height of 1,250 feet above sea level, and commands **magnificent views** of the Harbour and City of Victoria, the mainland of China and the neighbouring islands.

TERMS STRICTLY MODERATE.

A steam launch will meet all passenger steamers on arrival.
For full particulars apply at the office, Victoria Hotel.

Wm. FARMER,   **DORABJEE & HINGKEE,**
Manager.   *Proprietors.*

WINDSOR HOTEL,
HONGKONG.

The finest building in the Colony, situated in the most central part of Queen's Road.

The Elegant Entrance Hall being open from floor to roof 90 feet above, ensures good ventilation and coolness in the hot season.

Whilst fronting on Queen's Road, the Hotel possesses the advantage of a magnificent view of the harbour from a handsome terrace and flower garden, covered in by awnings, and so making a pleasant summer lounge. The "Windsor" has sprung quickly into public favour. For Families it has no equal in Hongkong, Seventy magnificent Rooms, luxuriously furnished and each bedroom having its Bathroom attached.

A Hydraulic lift conveys guests to the different floors. Public and Private Parlours and Dining Rooms. Special apartments for Ladies.

Cuisine best in the East, under European supervision.

PAUL BOHM,
Manager & Proprietor.

MOUNT AUSTIN HOTEL

HONGKONG.

1,400 Feet above Sea Level.

———:o:———

Telegraphic Address:
EXCELSIOR, HONGKONG.
A.B.C. CODE.

TELEPHONE, No. 35.

THE best appointed and most comfortable Hotel out of Europe, situated in the most beautiful and healthy part of the Hill District, and close to the Mountain Tramways' Upper Terminus.

The accommodation comprises a spacious Dining Hall, Private Dining Rooms, Drawing, Reading, Smoking, Billiard and Private Sitting Rooms. Every Bed-Room commands a magnificent view and is provided with a separate Bath-Room and every convenience.

The Cuisine is under the personal superintendence of an experienced European Steward.

For full particulars apply to the Secretary, Nos. 38 & 40, Queen's Road Central, or to the Manager, Mount Austin Hotel.

CANTON

THE SHAMEEN HOTEL & LAND CO., LD.

BRITISH CONCESSION.

THIS FIRST CLASS HOTEL, admirably situated within a few minutes walk of the 'River Steamer Wharves,' is now open to receive Visitors.

The Bed-rooms are cool, airy and confortably furnished, and the spacious Dining-Room, Sitting Rooms, and accommodation generally will be found equal to the best Hotels in the Far East.

The Table D'Hôte is supplied with every luxury in season, and the cuisine is in experienced hands.

Wines, Spirits, Malt Liquors, &c., of the best quality only.

A WELL APPOINTED BILLIARD-ROOM.

OFFICE, 7 D'AGUILAR STREET.

HONGKONG.

BOA VISTA HOTEL,

BISHOP'S BAY,

MACAO.

—:o:—

TELEGRAPHIC ADDRESS :—" BOAVISTA," MACAO.

—:o:—

Proprietress: *Manager:*

Mrs. MARIA B. DOS REMEDIOS.   Mr. L. M. DOS REMEDIOS.

—:o:—

THIS HOTEL IS SITUATED ON THE SEA SHORE IN ONE OF THE BEST AND HEALTHIEST PARTS OF MACAO, AND COMMANDS AN ADMIRABLE VIEW FACING THE SOUTH. ITS ACCOMMODATION IS UNSURPASSED IN THE FAR EAST.

EVERY COMFORT IS PROVIDED FOR VISITORS, WITH AN EXCELLENT CUISINE, AND WINES SPIRITS AND MALT LIQUORS OF THE BEST BRANDS.

HOT, COLD, SHOWER AND SEA WATER BATHS. LARGE AND WELL VENTILATED DINING, BILLIARD AND READING ROOMS, AND A WELL-SUPPLIED BAR.

FOR EUROPE, AMERICA, INDIA, AUSTRALIA, &c., AND FOR PRIVATE RESIDENTS AT THE OUTPORTS.

A COMPREHENSIVE AND COMPLETE RECORD OF THE
NEWS OF THE FAR EAST IS GIVEN IN THE

"Hongkong Weekly Press,"

WITH WHICH IS INCORPORATED

"THE CHINA OVERLAND TRADE REPORT."

SUBSCRIPTION, INCLUDING POSTAGE TO ANY PART OF THE WORLD, $10 PER ANNUM.

THE CHRONICLE AND DIRECTORY

FOR

CHINA, JAPAN, STRAITS, INDO-CHINA, &c.

ISSUED ANNUALLY FOR OVER THIRTY YEARS.

12 MAPS AND PLANS.

THE DIRECTORY covers the whole of the Ports and Cities of the Far East, from Penang to Vladivostock, in which Europeans reside.

Each Colony, Port, or Settlement is prefaced by a DESCRIPTION, carefully revised each year, some of which will serve as accurate GUIDES for the Tourist, giving every detail in connection with the places, their History, Topography, &c., &c.

The Information afforded in these Descriptions alone would suffice to fill an ordinary volume, consisting of over EIGHTY highly interesting articles, packed with facts concisely set out, and containing statistics of the TRADE of each Country and Port.

The CHRONICLE and DIRECTORY was years ago universally pronounced to be the cheapest work of the kind anywhere published, and although enlarged and improved in every way the price remains the same, notwithstanding the fall in exchange.

The size is Royal Octavo—Complete, with Maps and Plans, pp. 1130, $5.

It is published at the Office of the *Hongkong Daily Press*, and can be had from any Bookseller in Eastern Asia or from—

LONDON............ { Mr. F. ALGAR, 11, *Clement's Lane.*
{ Messrs. STREET & Co., 30, *Cornhill.*

PARIS ....Mr. L. H. RICHY, 66, *Rue Lafayette.*

GERMANY ....Messrs. MAHLAU & WALDESCHMIDT,
Frankfort o/M.

NEW YORK ....Mr. T. B. BROWNE, *353-5, Canal St.*

SAN FRAN'CO ...Mr. L. P. FISHER, 21, *Merchants' Exchange.*

SYDNEY .... }
MELBOURNE ... } Messrs. GORDON & GOTCH.

CALCUTTA` ....Messrs. W. NEWMAN & Co.

THE CHINA FIRE INSURANCE CO., LD.

CAPITAL - - - $2,000,000

PAID-UP CAPITAL $400,000   RESERVE FUND, 1893, $825,000

DIRECTORS:

H. HOPPIUS, Esq.	Messrs. Siemssen & Co., (*Chairman*).	
H. L. DALRYMPLE, Esq. ..	Messrs. Birley, Dalrymple & Co.	
A. G. WOOD, Esq.	Messrs. Gibb, Livingston & Co.	
A. McCONACHIE, Esq. ..	Messrs. Gilman & Co.	
D. R. SASSOON, Esq.	Messrs. David Sassoon, Sons, & Co.	
C. JANTZEN, Esq.	Messrs. Melchers & Co.	
J. KRAMER, Esq.	Messrs. Arnhold, Karberg & Co.	

AUDITORS:

J. H. COX, Esq., Hongkong. | ROBT. LYALL, Esq., Hongkong.

BANKERS:

THE HONGKONG & SHANGHAI BANKING CORPORATION.

HEAD OFFICE, No. 2, Queen's Road, HONGKONG.

JAS. B. COUGHTRIE,
Secretary.

CALDBECK, MACGREGOR & CO.

——:o:——

WINES, SPIRITS, & BEER MERCHANTS.

ESTABLISHED 1864.

SHANGHAI, 7, Foochow Road.

HONGKONG, 13, Queen's Road.

LONDON, 101, Leadenhall Street.

GLASGOW, Dixon Street, St. Enoch's Square.

ESTABLISHED 1864.   **Agencies:—**

Canton, Amoy, Taiwanfoo, Foochow, Hankow and Tientsin.

HOMEWARD PASSENGERS BY THE PACIFIC ROUTE

*ARE RECOMMENDED TO SEND THEIR HEAVY BAGGAGE
IN ADVANCE AS CARGO via SUEZ CANAL,*

TO THE CARE OF

HENRY S. KING & Co., LONDON.

THEIR AGENTS AT

HONGKONG, SHANGHAI and YOKOHAMA,

ARE

KELLY & WALSH, LIMITED,

WHO WILL UNDERTAKE THE SHIPMENT OF HOMEWARD
CARGO AND BAGGAGE

TO

Henry S. King & Co.,
LONDON.

HONGKONG, CANTON AND MACAO
STEAMBOAT Co., LD.

——:o:——

SAILINGS.

To **Canton.**—Every Morning, except Sunday, at 8 and every Evening, except Saturday, at 5.30.

From **Canton.**—Every Morning and Evening, except Sunday, at about 8 a.m. and about 5 p.m.

To **Macao.**—Each Weekday at 2 p.m.

From **Macao.**—Each Weekday at 8 a.m.

From **Canton** to **Macao.**—Every Tuesday, Thursday and Saturday, at about 8 a.m.

From **Macao** to **Canton.**—Every Monday, Wednesday and Friday, at 7.30 a.m.

The Times of departure will be adhered to as strictly as possible but are subject to alteration to suit the tides at Canton and Macao.

FARES.

To **Canton.**—Single $5. Return $10. Booking fee to ensure a berth by Night Steamer $1.

To **Macao.**—Single $3. Return $6 by any Steamer or $5 for Return by first Steamer.

From **Canton** to **Macao,** or *vice versa* $3 each way.

CIRCULAR Tickets, available either via Canton or via Macao, $11.

MEALS (inclusive of table Wine), $1.50 each.

Tickets and further information may be obtained at the Office of the Company, 18, Bank Buildings, Queen's Road, (entrance from Wyndham Street).

Hongkong, 27th April, 1893.

Lane, Crawford & Co.

QUEEN'S ROAD and PRAYA CENTRAL.

------ :o: ------

GENERAL STOREKEEPERS

AND IMPORTERS OF

EUROPEAN AND AMERICAN GOODS.

TOURISTS CAN OBTAIN THE FOLLOWING:—

COMPLETE OUTFITS
FIRST CLASS TAILORING
HOSIERY AND UNDERWEAR
SUN HATS AND SUN UMBRELLAS
SUN GLASSES AND BINOCULARS
RUBBER SEA BOOTS AND DECK
    SHOES
WALKING BOOTS AND SHOES
TRAVELLING TRUNKS, STRAPS, &c.
PRESERVED PROVISIONS
TRAVELLERS' COOKING STOVES
TRAVELLERS' READING LAMPS
CAMP FURNITURE AND FITTINGS

REVOLVERS AND FIREARMS
PLAYING CARDS AND GAMES
TRAVELLING CHESS SETS
ARTISTS COLOURS, &c.
NOTE BOOKS AND DIARIES
TRAVELLING INKSTANDS
TOILET REQUISITES
WATERPROOF GARMENTS
TRAVELLING RUGS
DECK CHAIRS AND HAMMOCKS
FLASKS, BOOKS, &c.
PIPES AND SMOKER'S SUNDRIES
MANILA CIGARS AND CHEROOTS.

LANE, CRAWFORD & Co.
HONGKONG.

CAMPBELL, MOORE & CO.,

LIMITED

(UNDER THE HONGKONG HOTEL)

ENTRANCES IN PEDDER'S STREET AND THE HONGKONG HOTEL.

Fashionable Hair Dressers, Wig Makers,

AND

PERFUMERS,

LADIES' HAIR TRIMMED AND SHAMPOOED AT THEIR RESIDENCES.

ALL KINDS OF HAIR WORK FOR LADIES, MADE TO ORDER

A LARGE ASSORTMENT OF TOILET REQUISITES FOR SALE,

PARTICULAR ATTENTION PAID TO RESETTING RAZORS.

AFONG,

PHOTOGRAPHER,

HAS FOR SALE A LARGER AND MORE COMPLETE

COLLECTION OF VIEWS

than any other Establishment in the Empire of China, and has quite recently added to it some NEW SELECTIONS of VIEWS and PHOTOS, of NATIVE TYPES, copies of which are obtainable in his *Studio* or at

Messrs. KELLY & WALSH, Limited.

IVORY MINIATURES of Superior Quality and of Excellent and High Finish.

He also undertakes to execute PERMANENT ENLARGEMENTS of PHOTOS, and VIEWS, and to reproduce the same on PAPER, CANVAS or OPAL.

INSTANTANEOUS VIEWS, GROUPS and PORTRAITS of different sizes are taken in any state of the weather, and all Permanent Processes are executed on MODERATE TERMS.

STUDIO, ICE HOUSE ROAD.
HONGKONG.

Queen's Road.] **CURIO!!** [*Hongkong Hotel!!!*

KUHN & CO.

CURIO!! **CURIO!!**

THE ORIENTAL FINE ART DEPOT!

BY APPOINTMENT. | **ESTABLISHED, 1869.** | HONGKONG.

———:o:———

JAPANESE AND CHINESE

WORKS OF ART

BEING THE

OLDEST & MOST RELIABLE ESTABLISHMENT

IN THE

EAST.

—:o:—

Our long experience and thorough knowledge of the trade, our special sources of supply, and our old System of buying for cash only, enable us to offer to all who may favour our Establishment, a *Bonâ-fide* advantage in every respect.

Wholesale and Retail orders promptly executed, and forwarded to any part of the World. Goods packed without charges.

DAKIN, CRUICKSHANK & CO.,

VICTORIA DISPENSARY,
HONGKONG.

DISPENSING CHEMISTS,
WHOLESALE, RETAIL AND MANUFACTURING
DRUGGISTS.
IMPORTERS OF
FINE BRANDS
OF
WINES, SPIRITS
AND
CIGARS.

MANUFACTURERS
OF
AERATED WATERS
BY STEAM POWER.

LONDON, HONGKONG, AMOY.
房藥大建德

HONGKONG TRADING COMPANY.

(NEXT DOOR TO THE HONGKONG DISPENSARY).

GENERAL DRAPERS

AND

OUTFITTERS.

TOURISTS' REQUISITES.

BEST QUALITIES AT MODERATE PRICES.

————:o:————

HONGKONG TRADING COMPANY,

No. 1, 3, 5 & 7, D'AQUILAR STREET.

R. J. REMEDIOS

WHOLESALE AND RETAIL DEALER IN FOREIGN AND COLONIAL POSTAGE STAMPS.

7, CHANCERY LANE,

HONGKONG.

Will be glad to call at any Visitor's room, at the Hongkong, Victoria, or Windsor House Hotels, to sell or exchange Stamps under the most favorable terms to Purchasers.

Purchasers will get stamps from him at 20 to 30 % cheaper than from shops in the town.

He will also buy used Postage Stamps in Large or Small Quantities for Cash.

W. Powell & Co.

GENERAL DRAPERS

AND

FURNISHERS

HONGKONG.

NEW GOODS BY NEARLY EVERY STEAMER.

===

E. RICCO & CIE.

66, QUEEN'S ROAD, HONGKONG.

——:o:——

GENERAL STORE-KEEPERS,

WINE & SPIRIT MERCHANTS.

NAVY CONTRACTORS,

——:o:——

HONGKONG & SHANGHAI.

THE HONGKONG HORSE REPOSITORY

(ESTABLISHED 1863.)

Proprietor, JOHN KENNEDY.

VETERINARY SURGEON AND FARRIER.

CARRIAGE BUILDER, SADDLER, AND HAY AND CORN DEALER

LIVERY STABLES.

Carriages and Ponies may be obtained on Hire at the shortest notice on very reasonable terms.

HORSES BROKEN TO SADDLE, SINGLE AND DOUBLE HARNESS.

The Hongkong Dairy.

PROPRIETOR, JOHN KENNEDY.

PRICE LIST FOR DAIRY PRODUCE.

MILK (ENGLISH COWS)	*Pint Bottles*	$0.09
" "	*Quart Bottles*	0.18
FRESH FARM BUTTER	*¼ ℔. Pat*	0.40
CREAM	*Per Pint*	0.50
CREAM CHEESES	*Each*	0.20
NEW LAID EGGS..	*Per Dozen*	0.25

Veal and English Sucking Pigs may occasionally be obtained on application. The best quality of everything guaranteed.

JOHN KENNEDY,
Proprietor.

HOTEL DE PEKING

PEKING.

CHINESE NAME—HAN-TAH-LEE. 亨達利飯店

L. TALLIEU, Proprietor.

OUTFITS
PROVIDED FOR JOURNEY
TO THE

GREAT WALL

AND

MING TOMBS.

•◦❖◦•

LLAMA FURS, SABLES,
ASTRACHANS,

AND OTHER SKINS SUPPLIED AT

CURRENT MARKET PRICES,

AS ALSO

THE CELEBRATED PEKING ENAMELS.

J. LLEWELLYN & CO., LTD.

:o:

WHOLESALE CHEMISTS

AND

DRUGGISTS,

AËRATED WATER MANUFACTURERS,

AND

DEALERS IN EVERY DESCRIPTION OF

PHARMACEUTICAL,

CHEMICAL & PHOTOGRAPHIC PREPARATIONS

AND APPARATUS.

Agents for

EASTMAN DRY PLATE & MATERIALS COMPANY.

KODAKS AND FILMS ALL SIZES.

:o:

Surgical Instruments, Patent Medicines

AND

DRUGGISTS' SUNDRIES.

:o:

MEDICAL HALL, SHANGHAI

CENTRAL HOTEL,

SHANGHAI.

———••o◇o••———

THIS long established SELECT Family Hotel, situated on the Bund, facing the River, in the Centre of the Settlements, has lately undergone Extensive Alterations, and is now fitted with the latest Modern Improvements, including Bath and Dressing-Rooms attached to Suites and Single Rooms, with Hot and Cold Water laid on, and heated to a Comfortable Temperature during Winter. Separate Rooms for Private Dinner Parties, etc.

The Hotel is Lighted throughout with the Electric Light.

An Assistant will attend on Passengers arriving by all Mail Steamers.

J. E. REILLY,
Proprietor.

N.B.—TELEGRAPHIC ADDRESS:
CENTRAL, SHANGHAI.

CANADIAN PACIFIC RAILWAY CO'S.
ROYAL MAIL STEAMSHIP LINE.

The FAST ROUTE BETWEEN CHINA, JAPAN, AND EUROPE
viâ
CANADA AND THE UNITED STATES.
CALLING AT
SHANGHAI, NAGASAKI, KOBE, YOKOHAMA AND VICTORIA, B.C.

"**EMPRESS OF INDIA**,"   6,000 *tons*.   10,000 *Horse Power*.
"**EMPRESS OF CHINA**,"   6,000 *tons*.   10,000 *Horse Power*.
"**EMPRESS OF JAPAN**,"   6,000 *tons*.   10,000 *Horse Power*.

THE STEAMERS of this Line pass through the famous INLAND SEA of JAPAN, and call at VICTORIA, B.C., to land and embark Passengers.

The Mountain Scenery on the Canadian Pacific Railway surpasses that of any other Trans-Continental Route.

Passengers Booked to all the principal points in Canada and the United States, and also through to Great Britian and the Continent of Europe, at Current Rates, with Passenger's choice of Atlantic Line.

Return Tickets.—Time limit for prepaid Return Tickets is reckoned from the date of embarkation to the date of rejoining the Canadian Pacific Railway Co's. Steamer on the return journey.

Special Tickets (*first class only*) are granted to Missionaries, Members of the Naval, Military, Diplomatic and Civil Services, and to European Officials in the services of China and Japan.

The Canadian Pacific Railway is the only Trans-Continental Line extending from the Pacific to the Atlantic Seaboard, and running its own Sleeping Coaches through without change. The Cars and Mountain Hotels on this Route are owned by the Company and their appointment and Cuisine are unexcelled.

The Steamers on the Pacific and all Day, Sleeping, and Dining Cars are comfortably heated by Steam during the Winter Season.

For further information as to Passage and Freight,

Apply to—
THE COMPANY'S OFFICES,

Pedder Street,
HONGKONG.

CHEMISTS BY APPOINTMENT.

A. S. WATSON & CO. LD.

司 公 臣 屈

ANALYSTS,

FAMILY and DISPENSING CHEMISTS,

WHOLESALE & RETAIL DRUGGISTS,

PERFUMERS, PATENT MEDICINE VENDORS,

DRUGGISTS' SUNDRYMEN, CIGAR DEALERS,

Wine & Spirit Merchants,

AND

AËRATED WATER MAKERS.

THE HONGKONG DISPENSARY,

房 藥 大 港 香

ESTABLISHED, A.D. 1841.

A. S. WATSON & Co., Ld.

THE HONGKONG DISPENSARY, Hongkong.
THE SHANGHAI PHARMACY, 24, Nanking Road, Shanghai.
BOTICA INGLESA, 14, Escolta, Manila.
THE CANTON DISPENSARY, Canton.
THE DISPENSARY, Foochow.
THE HONGKONG DISPENSARY, Hankow.
THE HONGKONG DISPENSARY, Tientsin.
LONDON OFFICE, 8, Fenchurch Buildings, E.C.

ASTOR HOUSE,

Telegraphic Address:
A.B.C. Code.
"JANSEN"

SHANGHAI.

————•o◊o•————

D. C. JANSEN, *Proprietor.*

THE OLDEST HOTEL BUSINESS IN THE FAR EAST.

ESTABLISHED 1858.   ENLARGED 1876.

Now added 24 additional Bed-Rooms, each with Verandah and adjoining Bath-Room with Hot and Cold Water service—new Dining-Room arrangements, new Bar-Room, new Billiard-Room; Ladies' Sitting-Room, Gentlemen's Sitting-Room, Reading-Room with Home and Local Papers, Private Dining-Rooms.

Hotel Servant boards all Incoming Steamers.

The Proprietor's long residence in China enables him to give special information about trips to Peking, Hankow, Ichang Gorges—or house-boat excursions through Kiangsu " The Garden of the Empire" the scene of Chinese Gordon's exploits, a sail along the Grand Canal, a visit to Soochow, to Hang chow (the Kinsai of Marco Polo). House-boats fitted out and guns and dogs obtained for shooting parties.

COOK'S COUPONS TAKEN.

250HP28/60